THE COMPLETE BOOK OF

CHINESE COOKING

THE COMPLETE BOOK OF
CHINESE COOKING

Edited by
Veronica Sperling & Christine McFadden

PARRAGON

First published in Great Britain in 1996 by
Parragon Book Service Ltd
Unit 13–17
Avonbridge Trading Estate
Atlantic Road
Avonmouth
Bristol BS11 9QD

ISBN: 0-75252-057-1

Printed in Italy

Produced by Haldane Mason, London

Acknowledgements
Art Direction: Ron Samuels
Design: Digital Artworks Partnership Ltd

Material contained in this book has previously appeared in
Chinese Cantonese Cooking and *Chinese Szechuan Cooking* by Deh-Ta Hsiung
Vegetarian Chinese Cooking and *Microwave Meals* by Wendy Lee
Wok Cooking by Rosemary Wadey
Thai Cooking by Carol Bowen
Quick & Easy Meals by Carole Handslip

Contents

CHINESE CUISINE

From the hot, spicy dishes of Szechuan to the aromatic crispy duck of Beijing, the cooking of China offers a fascinating range of delicious dishes for you to create in your own kitchen. Once you have mastered one or two simple basic principles, you'll appreciate the speed and ease with which Chinese food can be cooked, whether it is for a complete meal or as an accompaniment to your normal food.

THE CHINESE DIET

With its wealth of foodstuffs and distinctive regional cooking styles, it's little wonder that China claims to have the world's most diverse cuisine. Yet the fundamental character of Chinese cooking remains the same throughout the land: from Peking in the north to Canton in the south, and from Shanghai in the east to Szechuan in the west, different ingredients are prepared, cooked and served in accordance with centuries-old principles. Some of the cooking methods may vary a little from one region to another, and the emphasis on seasonings may differ, but basically dishes from different regions are all unmistakably 'Chinese'.

A HEALTHY OPTION

The variety of Chinese cooking appeals to people in every corner of the globe, not only because of the range of unusual and exotic ingredients but because the daily diet is one of the healthiest in the world. It is based largely on vegetables and carbohydrates (such as rice or noodles) with only a little fish or meat. Dairy products are not used.

THE VEGETARIAN ELEMENT

Widespread poverty means that many people are unable to afford meat, and many follow a vegetarian diet for religious reasons. In addition, the selection of vegetables available in the markets has increased in recent years as China's peasants have been encouraged to grow their own crops. But even when they have the choice, the Chinese have many reasons for eating more vegetarian food than other kinds. They recognize not only that a mainly vegetarian diet is the healthiest way to eat, but that it is also more economical to use the land for growing vegetables and rice than for grazing livestock, as the crops will feed infinitely more people.

REGIONAL COOKING

Being such a vast country – about the same size as the United States – China encompasses a number of different climates. Even though it lies mainly within the temperate zone both geographically and climatically, the regions are widely diverse. From the Tibetan Plateau in the west (3,600 m/12,000 ft), the country descends continually eastwards until it arrives at the Yangtze flood plain. It is the diversity of the countryside that has given rise to the wide variety of produce and the great range of regional cooking styles. China breaks down into four distinct regions, each of which has its own style of cuisine and specialities.

Cantonese (Southern School)

This is the best-known cuisine in the western world because of the large numbers of Chinese who emigrated from Canton to Europe and America in the nineteenth century. Also, because Canton was the first Chinese port opened for trade, it is the most influenced by foreign contact and offers the widest variety of food. Light and subtle flavourings are used and the food is less fatty than in other regions. The region is famous for its seafood specialities as well as its sweet and sour dishes and crispy pork recipes.

Peking (Northern School)

The staple food is mainly wheat, corn and maize, rather than rice, with an emphasis on noodles, dumplings and pancakes. Due to the harsh winter, many food products are preserved by drying, smoking or pickling.

Szechuan (Western School)

The Szechuan cuisine is characterized by its dependence on strong flavourings and hot spices such as red chillies, Szechuan peppercorns, ginger and garlic. Pungent vegetables such as garlic, onions and spring onions (scallions) are used in large quantities. Nuts add richness and flavour to dishes, while aromatic ground rice and sesame seeds are often used to coat meat prior to deep-frying or stir-frying. Sesame paste is often the principal ingredient in sauces. The region is also noted for its food preservation techniques, which include salting, drying, smoking and pickling, probably because the humid climate makes it difficult to keep food fresh.

Shanghai (Eastern School)

This region is rich in fruit and vegetables, and is well known for its vegetarian cuisine as well as its fresh fish. Sugar and oil are used in large quantities, earning the area a reputation for rich food.

THE PRINCIPLES OF CHINESE COOKING

What distinguishes Chinese cooking from all other food cultures is the emphasis on the harmonious blending of colour, aroma, flavour and texture, both in a single dish and in all the dishes which make up the meal. Consciously or unconsciously, Chinese cooks, from the housewife to the professional chef, all work to this ancient Taoist principle of Yin and Yang in which balance and contrast are the key.

In order to achieve this, two most important factors should be observed, that is, heat and timing – the degree of heat and duration of cooking, which means the right cooking method for the right food. This is why the size and shape of the cut ingredient must, first of all, be suitable for a particular method of cooking. For instance, ingredients for quick stir-frying should be cut into small, thin slices or shreds of uniform size, never into large, thick chunks. This is not just for the sake of appearance, but also because ingredients of the same size and shape require about the same amount of cooking time.

Bear these general points in mind when you cook Chinese food and you will find it surprisingly easy to create delicious dishes that are also a visual delight.

The recipes in this book have been designed to achieve exactly this. They are quick and simple to prepare and they mostly use ingredients obtainable from supermarkets. Occasionally, you may need to visit a Chinese food store to find one or two ingredients. Some of the recipes have been adapted for the vegetarian from traditional Chinese recipes, and others are vegetarian dishes that have been developed to suit the Western kitchen.

CHINESE MEALS

Meal times in China are often family gatherings at which many different dishes are served. A wide range of ingredients is used, but the different flavours of the many dishes are always made to work together. The meal is served all at once, including the soup. Unlike the Western convention, the Chinese never serve an individual dish to each person; all the dishes on the table are shared.

The Chinese do not usually have desserts to finish off a meal, except at banquets and special occasions. Sweet dishes are usually served in between main meals as snacks, but fruit is refreshing at the end of a big meal.

MENU PLANNING

When planning a menu for a shared meal, allow one dish per person. For example, if you are cooking for only two or three people, serve one main dish with one vegetable side dish and one rice or noodle dish, plus a soup if desired. For an informal meal for four to six people, serve four dishes plus soup and rice; for a formal dinner for approximately the same number of people, allow a range of six to eight dishes. Always increase the number of dishes rather than the quantity of ingredients when cooking for many people, as this will give more variety and contrast of taste, colour and flavour on the table.

Do not choose too many dishes that need a lot of last-minute preparation or have to be served immediately, such as stir-fries. Vary the dishes so that some may be prepared in advance, and then you too can enjoy the meal and not spend all evening in the kitchen.

TEA DRINKING

In China, tea is unlikely to be drunk during the actual meal, as it is generally the custom to place a bowl of clear soup on the table instead for the duration of the meal. Tea is then served at the end of the meal as it is considered to be both refreshing and invigorating.

Tea has been known as a drink in China certainly for more than 2,000 years and probably much earlier. However, it was not until the eighth century that tea became a common drink, popular with all classes of people. Today, tea drinking is a part of everyday life in China and a pot of strong tea is kept warm all day to provide a regular supply. To the tea connoisseur, the tradition of tea drinking is, as it has always been through the ages, akin to a religious ritual and a return to nature and purity. Ideally, preparing tea should be carried out under immaculate and tranquil conditions. The setting is especially important and should be as peaceful as possible; in fact, the ideal spot is considered to be on a mountain so that, as an additional benefit, mountain water is used for the tea.

WINE

Many European and New World wines blend well with Chinese food, particularly the light, dry whites and lighter Burgundy-style reds. Chinese wine is an acquired taste. Being mostly made with fermented rice, it has a very different flavour from wine made with grapes. The best-known Chinese wine is called Shaoxing, which is also used in cooking.

GLOSSARY OF INGREDIENTS

The list covers the most commonly used ingredients in Chinese cooking. These ingredients are becoming much more widely available, particularly in the supermarkets, health food shops and Chinese stores. Substitutes can often be used for the more unusual ingredients.

Baby sweetcorn (corn)

Baby sweetcorn cobs have a wonderfully sweet flavour and irresistible texture. They are available both fresh and canned.

Bamboo shoots

Available in cans only. Once opened, the contents may be kept in fresh water in a covered jar in the refrigerator for up to a week.

Bean-sprouts

Fresh bean-sprouts, from mung or soya beans, are widely available from oriental stores and supermarkets. They can be kept in the refrigerator for two to three days.

Bean sauce

Available in black or yellow, bean sauce is made from crushed salted soya beans mixed with flour and spices (such as ginger or chilli) to make a thickish paste. It is used for flavouring dishes or as a condiment. The sauce is sold in cans or jars and once opened should be stored in the refrigerator.

Black beans

Salted fermented soya beans, available in packets or cans.

Chilli bean sauce

Fermented bean paste mixed with hot chillies and other seasonings. Sold in jars, some sauces are quite mild, but others are very hot. You will have to try out the various brands to see which one is to your taste.

Chillies

These can be red or green, and come in a variety of sizes – the smaller the chilli, the hotter it is, and dried chillies are often hotter than fresh. Take care when handling them, as chilli juice stings; avoid touching your eyes and always wash your hands thoroughly afterwards. Discard the seeds, as these are the hottest part.

Chilli oil

A very hot chilli-flavoured red oil; use sparingly. You can make your own by adding a few dried chillies to a small bottle of oil. Leave them to soak for a few days to allow the flavour to develop.

Chilli sauce

Very hot sauce made from chillies, vinegar, sugar and salt. Usually sold in bottles and should be used sparingly in cooking or as a dip. Tabasco sauce can be used as a substitute if you do not happen to have the real thing.

Chinese leaves

Also known as Chinese cabbage, there are two widely available varieties to be found in supermarkets and greengrocers. The most common is pale green with a tightly wrapped, elongated head. Roughly two-thirds of the cabbage consists of crunchy-textured stem. The other variety has a shorter, fatter head with curlier, pale yellow or green leaves with white stems.

Coriander (cilantro)

Fresh coriander leaves, also known as Chinese parsley or

cilantro, have a distinctive flavour. Coriander (cilantro) is widely used in Chinese cooking. It can be chopped and added to sauces and stuffing. The feathery leaves make an attractive garnish. Parsley can be used as a substitute.

Dried Chinese mushrooms

Highly fragrant dried mushrooms which add a special flavour to Chinese dishes. There are many different varieties, but shiitake are the best. They are not cheap, but a small amount will go a long way, and they will keep indefinitely in an airtight jar. Soak them in warm water for 20–30 minutes (or in cold water for several hours), squeeze dry and discard the hard stalks (stems) before use.

Egg noodles

There are many varieties of egg noodles in China, ranging from flat, broad ribbons to long, narrow strands. Both dried and fresh egg noodles are readily available.

Five-spice powder

A mixture of star anise, fennel seeds, cloves, cinnamon bark and Szechuan pepper. It is very pungent so should be used sparingly. It will keep in an airtight container indefinitely.

Garlic

A primary seasoning in Chinese food that not only adds flavour but has health-giving properties. Garlic may be chopped, crushed or pickled and is very often used in sauces and stuffings. Store garlic in a cool, dry area, not in the fridge where it will go mouldy.

Ginger root

Fresh ginger root, sold by the weight, should be peeled and then sliced, finely chopped or shredded before use. It will keep for several weeks in a dry, cool place. Dried ginger powder is not a good substitute.

Hoisin sauce

Also known as barbecue sauce, this is made from soy beans, sugar, flour, vinegar, salt, garlic, chilli and sesame seed oil. Sold in cans or jars, it will keep in the refrigerator for several months.

Lemon grass

An aromatic herb, available as fresh stems or dried as powder. Chop or slice the lower part of the stem to use.

Lily flowers

Also known as golden needles, these are dried lily-flower buds. Soak in water before use.

Lotus leaves

Leaves of the lotus plant. They are very large and sold dried. Soak in hot water before use. These are often used as a shell in which other ingredients are cooked, such as steamed rice.

Noodles

Made from rice, pulses or wheat. There is a large variety available, all of which can be interchanged in recipes. Cook according to packet instructions as times vary from one type to another.

Oils

The most commonly used oil in Chinese cooking is peanut (groundnut) oil. It has a light flavour and can be heated without smoking to a higher temperature than most oils. It is therefore especially useful for stir-frying and deep-frying. Rape or sunflower oils are also popular, while butter is never used, and lard and chicken fat only occasionally.

Oyster sauce

A thickish soy-based sauce used as a flavouring in Cantonese cooking. Sold in bottles, it will keep in the refrigerator for months.

Plum sauce

Plum sauce has a unique, fruity flavour – a sweet and sour sauce with a difference.

Rice vinegar

There are two basic types of rice vinegar. Red vinegar is made from fermented rice and has a distinctive dark colour and depth of flavour. White vinegar is stronger in flavour as it is distilled from rice wine.

Rice wine

Chinese rice wine, made from glutinous rice, is also known as yellow wine (*huang jiu* or *chiew* in Chinese), because of its golden colour. The best variety, from south-east China, is called Shao Hsing or Shaoxing. A good dry or medium sherry can be an acceptable substitute.

Sesame oil

Aromatic oil sold in bottles and widely used as a finishing touch, added to dishes just before serving. The refined yellow sesame oil sold in Middle Eastern stores is not so aromatic, has less flavour and therefore is not a very satisfactory substitute.

Sesame seeds

These add texture and a nutty flavour to dishes. Dry-fry to add colour and accentuate the flavour.

Sherry

If rice wine is difficult to obtain, a good quality dry pale sherry can be used instead. Cream or sweet sherry should not be substituted.

Soy sauce

Sold in bottles or cans, this popular Chinese sauce is used both for cooking and at the table. Light soy sauce has more flavour than the sweeter, dark soy sauce, which gives the food a rich, reddish colour.

Straw mushrooms

Grown on beds of rice straw, hence the name, straw mushrooms have a pleasant slippery texture and a subtle taste. Canned straw mushrooms should be rinsed and drained after opening.

Szechuan peppercorns

Also known as *farchiew*, these are wild reddish-brown peppercorns from Szechuan. More aromatic but less hot than either white or black peppercorns, they give a unique and delicious flavour to a variety of dishes.

Szechuan preserved vegetable

This is a speciality of Szechuan province. It is the root of a special variety of the mustard green pickled in salt and hot chilli. Sold in cans, once opened it can be stored in a sealed jar in the refrigerator for months.

Tofu (bean curd)

This custard-like preparation of puréed and pressed yellow soya beans is exceptionally high in protein. Tofu (bean curd) has a distinctive texture but a bland flavour. It is usually sold in two forms: in cakes about 7.5 cm/3 inches square and 2.5 cm/1 inch thick or as a semi-thick jelly. There is also a dried form, which is sold in oriental and health food stores. For solid tofu (bean curd), use a sharp knife to cut the required amount into cubes or shreds. Cook carefully as it will break up if stirred too much. Tofu (bean curd) will keep for a few days in the refrigerator if put in a sealed container and submerged in water.

Water chestnuts

The roots of the plant *Heleocharis tuberosa*. Also known as horse's hooves in China on account of their appearance before the skin is peeled off. They are available fresh or in cans. Canned water chestnuts retain only part of the texture, and even less of the flavour of fresh ones. They will keep for a month in the refrigerator in a covered jar, changing the water every two or three days.

Wood ears

Also known as cloud ears, this is a dried black fungus. Sold in plastic bags in oriental stores, they should be soaked in cold or warm water for 20 minutes, then rinsed in fresh water before use. Wood ears have a crunchy texture and mild but subtle flavour. Fresh 'Jews ears' are a good substitute.

Wonton skins or wrappers

These are made from flour, egg and water. They can be deep-fried and served with a dipping sauce, or filled prior to deep-frying, steaming or boiling. Buy them ready-made or make your own. Layers of filo pastry make a reasonable substitute. They can be kept frozen for up to six months.

EQUIPMENT

Chinese utensils are of an ancient design and are usually made of inexpensive materials. They have been in continuous use for thousands of years and do serve a special function. Their more sophisticated and expensive Western counterparts sometimes prove rather inadequate in contrast.

Chinese cleaver

Good, strong, sharp kitchen knives are more than adequate but it is worth trying to work with a Chinese cleaver. The wide blade looks clumsy, but the corner of the blade can do anything the point of a knife can do. Also, the blade can be used to carry the chopped ingredients to the cooking pot.

Cleavers vary in weight and thickness of blade. The heavier type is used for chopping through bones, while the lighter, sharper type is ideal for delicate, precision work.

Chopsticks

Does Chinese food taste any better when eaten with chopsticks? This is not merely an aesthetic question, but also a practical point, partly because all Chinese food is prepared in such a way that it is easily picked up by chopsticks.

Learning to use chopsticks is quite easy – simply place one chopstick in the hollow between thumb and index finger and rest its lower end below the first joint of the third finger. This chopstick remains stationary. Hold the other chopstick between the tips of the index and middle finger, steady its upper half against the base of the index finger, and use the tip of the thumb to keep it in place. To pick up food, move the upper chopstick with index and middle fingers. When eating rice and other difficult-to-hold foods, it is better to lift the bowl to the chin and then push the food into the mouth using the chopsticks as a type of shovel, as the Chinese do.

Chopsticks are also used in food preparation, as they make an excellent tool for stirring, whipping and beating the ingredients prior to cooking. They can be bought in most cookshops and from many Chinese restaurants.

Ladle and spatula

Wok sets usually consist of a pair of stirrers in the form of a ladle and spatula. Of the two, the flat ladle or scooper (as it is sometimes called) is more versatile. It is used by the Chinese cook for adding ingredients and seasonings to the wok, besides being a stirring implement.

Steamers

Steaming can be done in any covered pot large enough to take a plate placed on a rack set over boiling water. There should be space for the steam to circulate. The food is put on the plate and a well-fitting lid put on top. A wok with its own lid will serve very well. The traditional Chinese steamer is made of bamboo; the modern version is made of aluminium.

Bamboo steamers are particularly suited to the technique as the gaps in the bamboo allow excess steam to escape. They are designed to stand one on top of another, enabling you to cook several dishes at the same time. They can be bought in a range of sizes at Chinese speciality shops or good cookware shops.

Wok

The round-bottomed iron wok conducts and retains heat evenly. Because of its shape, the ingredients always return to the centre, where the heat is most intense, however vigorously you stir. The wok is also ideal for deep-frying – its conical shape requires far less oil than a flat-bottomed deep-fryer. It has more depth (which means more heat) and more cooking surface (which means more food can be cooked at one go). Besides being a frying-pan (skillet), a wok is also used for braising, steaming, boiling and poaching – in other words, the whole spectrum of Chinese cooking methods can be executed in one single utensil.

It is essential that a new iron wok is seasoned properly before use. Prepare it by washing thoroughly in hot water and detergent then drying it well. To season, put the wok over a gentle heat and, when the metal heats up, wipe over the entire inner surface with a pad of paper towels that you have first dipped in oil. Repeat the process using fresh oiled paper until the paper stays clean.

Clean the wok after each use by washing it with water, using a mild detergent if necessary, and a soft cloth or brush. Do not scrub or use any abrasive cleaner as this will scratch the surface. Dry thoroughly with paper towels or over a low heat, then wipe the surface all over with a little oil. This forms a sealing layer to protect the surface of the wok from moisture and thus helps to prevent it from rusting.

GARNISHES

Chinese food should always be pleasing to the eye as well as the palate. The dishes can be intricately decorated with delicately cut vegetables, adding colour as well as a finishing touch. The garnishes can be as simple or elaborate as you wish, depending on time and patience. The more simple garnishes could be sprigs of fresh or chopped herbs such as coriander (cilantro), chervil or chives, shreds of spring onion (scallion), chilli, lemon zest or radish, or twists of lime or lemon. Some more elaborate garnishes are described below. Experiment with both for the best results.

Cucumber fans

Cut a piece of cucumber about 7.5 cm/3 inches long and divide this in half lengthways. Lay a piece of cucumber cut side down and, using a small, sharp knife, cut thin slices along the length to within 1 cm/½ inch of the end. Carefully turn alternate slices over in half and tuck in. Place in iced water until required.

Carrot flowers

Peel the carrot. Using a sharp knife, make about five or six tiny V-shaped cuts along the length. Then cut into slices: the V-shapes will ensure each slice looks like a flower petal.

Fresh chilli flowers

Trim the tip of the chilli but do not remove the skin. Make four cuts lengthways from the stem of the chilli to the tip to make four sections. Remove and discard any seeds. Soak the chillies in cold water – they will flower in the water.

Prawn (shrimp) crackers

These are compressed slivers of prawn (shrimp) and flour paste which expand into large, translucent crisps when deep-fried.

Radish flowers

Trim each end of the radish. Using a sharp knife, make V-shaped cuts around the top and remove the cut parts to expose the whites of the radish.

Radish roses

For radish roses, trim the ends, then hold the knife flat to the radish skin and make short vertical cuts around the sides, as if you were shaving off the outer skin, but without detaching each 'petal'. Plunge straight into iced water.

Tomato roses

For tomato roses, peel off the skin of a tomato using a sharp knife in one long strip. Curl the skin into a circle.

COOKING TECHNIQUES

Chinese food generally takes much longer to prepare than it does to cook, so it is very important to prepare each dish as much in advance as possible. Have all the vegetables chopped and sauces blended before you start cooking.

Chopping

Cut the ingredients into small, uniformly sized pieces to ensure that the food cooks evenly. Shredding vegetables thinly and slicing them diagonally ensures fast cooking, as it increases the area in contact with the hot oil.

Stir-frying

This is the method of cooking most commonly associated with Chinese cuisine. The correct piece of equipment for this is a wok (see page 13) as it gives the best results. However, any large frying-pan (skillet) or heavy saucepan will do.

Stir-frying with a wok is a very healthy way to cook, as it uses very little oil and preserves the nutrients in the food. It is very important that the wok is very hot before you begin to cook. This can be tested by holding your hand flat about 7.5 cm/3 inches over the base of the interior, when you will feel the heat radiating from it. The success of stir-frying lies in having the wok at just the right temperature, and in ensuring correct timing when cooking the food.

Before cooking commences, ensure that all the required ingredients are prepared, ready to be added to the wok the instant the oil is the right heat. Cooking at too low a temperature or for too long will produce inferior results.

Add a small amount of oil to the wok and heat it, then add, in stages, the various ingredients to be cooked – those requiring longer cooking go in first, while those that require only very little cooking go in last.

Using a long-handled metal or wooden spoon or flat scoop, constantly stir the ingredients for a very short time. This ensures that all the ingredients come into contact with the hot oil so the natural juices of the food are sealed in, leaving it crisp and colourful. The technique also ensures that all the ingredients are evenly cooked. Stir-fried dishes look and taste best when served immediately.

Deep-frying

Use a wok, a deep-fryer or a heavy-based saucepan. When deep-frying in a wok, use enough oil to give a depth of about 5 cm/2 inches. Heat it over a moderate heat until you can see a faint haze of smoke rising before gently lowering in the food to be fried. Make sure the oil is up to temperature before adding the food so that the hot oil cooks the food quickly on the outside, forming a protective seal. If the oil is not hot enough, the food will act like a sponge and becoming soggy and greasy. Before frying the food, make sure that it is dry in order to prevent the oil from splattering. If the food has been marinated, let it drain well. If it is in batter, wait for it to stop dripping.

Cook the food in small batches so as not to overcrowd the wok or pan, as this can reduce the temperature of the oil and lead to unevenly cooked food. Always remove the food from the oil with a perforated spoon and drain thoroughly on paper towels to absorb any excess oil. Once it has been strained, cooking oil can be reused up to three times, but only for the same type of food.

Steaming

This is another very popular Chinese cooking method. There are two methods of steaming. In the first, the food is arranged on a plate or bowl which is then put inside a steamer on a perforated rack and placed over a large pot of boiling water. The plate or bowl can also be put inside a wok. The steam passes through the steamer and cooks the food. Larger items of food such as dumplings can be placed straight on to the rack or laid on cabbage leaves or soaked lotus leaves. The leaves not only prevent the food from falling through, but also add extra flavour.

In the second method, the bowl of ingredients is partially immersed in boiling water. The food is cooked partly by the boiling water and partly by the steam it produces.

Braising and red braising

This method is similar to Western braising and is generally used for cooking tougher cuts of meat and firm varieties of vegetables. The ingredients are stir-fried until lightly brown. Stock is added and brought to the boil. The heat is then reduced to simmering until cooking is complete. Red braising uses the same method but the food is braised in a reddish-brown liquid, such as soy sauce. This sauce can be re-used.

BASIC RECIPES

Common to many recipes are standard preparations such as stock, plain boiled rice and cornflour (cornstarch) paste. Dipping sauces are also served with many dishes.

Chinese Stock

This basic stock is used not only as the basis for soup-making, but also for general use in Chinese cooking. It will keep for up to 4–5 days in the refrigerator. Alternatively, it can be frozen in small containers and defrosted as required. These quantities make 2.5 litres/4 pints/10 cups.

750 g/1½ lb chicken pieces
750 g/1½ lb pork spare ribs
3.75 litres/6 pints/15 cups cold water
3–4 pieces ginger root, crushed
3–4 spring onions (scallions), each tied into a knot
3–4 tbsp Chinese rice wine or dry sherry

Trim off excess fat from the chicken and spare ribs, then chop them into large pieces. Put in a large pan with the water, ginger and spring onion (scallion) knots. Bring to the boil, and skim off the scum. Reduce the heat and simmer uncovered for at least 2–3 hours. Strain the stock, discarding the chicken, pork, ginger and spring onions (scallions). Pour back in the pan and add the wine. Bring to the boil, then simmer for 2–3 minutes. Allow to cool, then store in the refrigerator.

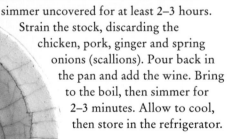

Cornflour (Cornstarch) Paste

Cornflour (cornstarch) paste is made by mixing 1 part cornflour (cornstarch) with about 1.5 parts of cold water. Stir until smooth. Use to thicken sauces.

Plain Rice

Use long-grain or patna rice, or better still, try Thai fragrant rice. This amount serves 4.

250 g/8 oz/1¼ cups long-grain rice
about 200 ml/7 fl oz/1 cup cold water
pinch of salt
½ tsp oil (optional)

Wash and rinse the rice just once. Place the rice in a saucepan and add just enough water so that there is no more than 2 cm/½ inch of water above the surface of the rice. Bring to the boil, add salt and oil (if using), and stir once to prevent the rice sticking to the bottom of the pan.

Reduce the heat to very, very low. Cover and cook for 15–20 minutes. Remove from the heat and let stand, covered, for 10 minutes or so. Fluff up the rice with a fork or spoon before serving.

DIPPING SAUCES

Traditional sauces for Chinese food include the following.

Sweet & Sour Sauce

A tasty sweet and sour sauce which goes well with many deep- fried foods. Store in a well-sealed container in the refrigerator. It will keep well.

2 tbsp ginger marmalade
2 tbsp orange marmalade
¼ tsp salt
1 tbsp white rice vinegar (or cider vinegar)
1 tbsp hot water

Combine all the ingredients in a small bowl, mixing well. Serve in a small bowl.

Salt & Pepper Sauce

A roasted salt and pepper mixture made with Szechuan peppercorns is found throughout China as a dip for deep-fried foods. The dry-roasting method brings out all the flavours of the peppercorns.

2 oz/50 g Szechuan peppercorns
3 oz/75 g coarse sea salt

Put a heavy frying-pan (skillet) over medium heat. Add the peppercorns and the salt and stir-fry until the mixture begins to brown. Remove the pan (skillet) from the heat and let the mixture cool. Grind the mixture in a grinder or with a pestle and mortar.

Spring Onion (Scallion) Sauce

Heated oil poured over the seasonings brings out their full flavour. The sauce goes well with meat and poultry dishes.

3 tbsp spring onions (scallions), chopped finely
3 tbsp fresh ginger root, grated finely
2 tsp salt
1 tsp light soy sauce
3 tbsp oil (peanut or sunflower)

Place the spring onions (scallions), ginger root, salt and soy sauce in a small heat-proof bowl. Put the oil into a small saucepan and heat over a moderate heat until it begins to smoke.

Remove the oil from the heat and pour over the seasonings. Leave the sauce to stand for at least 2–3 hours before using, to allow the flavours to blend.

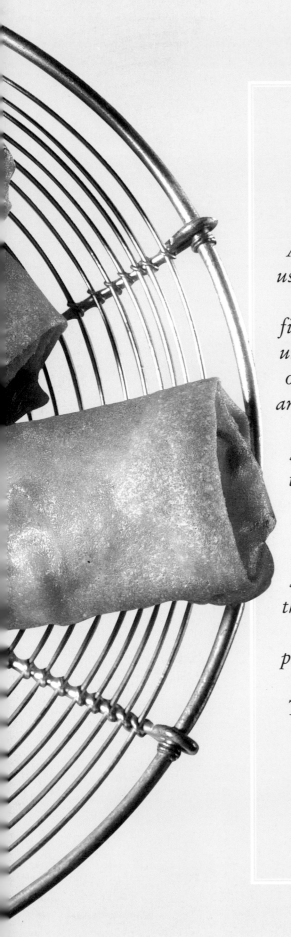

APPETIZERS

A selection of small portions of several different dishes usually starts the Chinese meal – just like hors d'oeuvres in the West. Many of these appetizers consist of tasty fillings enclosed in pastry-type wrappers which are fried until crisp. These are served with a simple dipping sauce of soy sauce, sherry and strips of spring onion (scallion) and chilli. Spicy deep-fried prawns (shrimp) or bite-sized spare ribs or pieces of chicken are also popular.

Serve an assortment of appetizers with a minimum of three different items, but remember not to have more than one of the same type of food. The ingredients should be chosen for their harmony and balance in colour, aroma, texture and flavour.

Snacks and appetizers are sold at many roadside stalls throughout China, and are bought and eaten by people as they go about their daily tasks. After dusk, the pavements are filled with groups of families and friends cooking, eating and selling many delicious meals.

This is an important part of their social lives, and is an enjoyable way of getting together and sharing food.

Crispy Wontons with Piquant Dipping Sauce

Mushroom-filled crispy wontons are served on skewers
with a chilli-flavoured dipping sauce.

SERVES 4

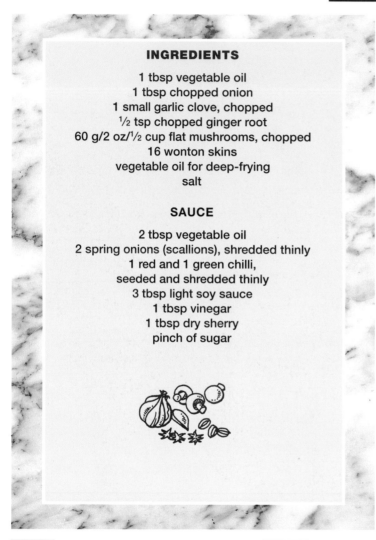

INGREDIENTS

1 tbsp vegetable oil
1 tbsp chopped onion
1 small garlic clove, chopped
½ tsp chopped ginger root
60 g/2 oz/½ cup flat mushrooms, chopped
16 wonton skins
vegetable oil for deep-frying
salt

SAUCE

2 tbsp vegetable oil
2 spring onions (scallions), shredded thinly
1 red and 1 green chilli,
seeded and shredded thinly
3 tbsp light soy sauce
1 tbsp vinegar
1 tbsp dry sherry
pinch of sugar

1 Heat the oil in a wok or frying pan (skillet). Add the onion, garlic and ginger root, and stir-fry for 2 minutes. Stir in the mushrooms and fry for a further 2 minutes. Season well with salt and leave to cool.

2 Place 1 teaspoon of the cooled mushroom filling in the centre of each wonton skin. Bring two opposite corners together to cover the mixture and pinch together to seal. Repeat with the remaining corners.

3 Thread the wontons on to 8 wooden skewers. Heat enough oil in a large saucepan to deep-fry the wontons in batches until golden and crisp. Remove with a perforated spoon and drain on paper towels.

4 To make the sauce, heat the oil in a small saucepan until quite hot, i.e. until a small cube of bread dropped in the oil browns in a few seconds. Put the spring onions (scallions) and chillies in a bowl and pour the hot oil slowly on top. Then mix in the remaining ingredients and serve with the crispy wontons.

Step *1*

Step *2*

Step *4*

Crispy Seaweed

Popular in many Chinese restaurants, this dish is served as a starter.
This 'seaweed' is in fact deep-fried spring greens.

SERVES 4

INGREDIENTS

250 g/8 oz spring greens
vegetable oil for deep-frying
1½ tsp caster (superfine) sugar
1 tsp salt
30 g/1 oz/¼ cup flaked (slivered) almonds

1 Wash the spring greens thoroughly. Trim off the excess tough stalks. Place on paper towels or a dry tea towel (dish cloth) and leave to drain thoroughly.

2 Using a sharp knife, shred the spring greens very finely then spread out the shreds on paper towels for about 30 minutes to dry.

3 Heat the oil in a wok or deep-fat fryer. Remove the pan from the heat and add the spring greens in batches. Return the pan to the heat and deep-fry until the greens begin to float to the surface and become translucent and crinkled. Remove with a perforated spoon, and drain on paper towels. Keep each batch warm.

4 Mix the sugar and salt together, sprinkle over the 'seaweed' and toss together to mix well.

5 Add the flaked (slivered) almonds to the hot oil and fry until lightly golden. Remove with a perforated spoon and drain on paper towels.

6 Serve the crispy 'seaweed' with the flaked (slivered) almonds.

Step *2*

Step *3*

Step *4*

Spring Rolls

Thin slices of vegetables are wrapped in pastry and deep-fried until crisp.
Spring roll wrappers are available from oriental shops and some supermarkets.

MAKES 12

INGREDIENTS

5 Chinese dried mushrooms
(or open-cup mushrooms)
1 large carrot
60 g/2 oz/1 cup canned bamboo shoots
2 spring onions (scallions)
60 g/2 oz Chinese leaves
2 tbsp vegetable oil
250 g/8 oz/4 cups bean-sprouts
1 tbsp soy sauce
12 spring roll wrappers
1 egg, beaten
vegetable oil for deep-frying
salt

1 Place the dried mushrooms in a small bowl and cover with warm water. Leave to soak for 20–25 minutes. Drain the mushrooms and squeeze out the excess water. Remove the tough centres and slice the mushrooms fairly thinly.

2 Cut the carrot and bamboo shoots into very thin julienne strips. Chop the spring onions (scallions) and shred the Chinese leaves.

3 Heat the 2 tablespoons of oil in a wok or frying pan (skillet). Add the mushrooms, carrot and bamboo shoots, and stir-fry for 2 minutes. Add the spring onions (scallions), Chinese leaves, bean-sprouts and soy sauce. Season with salt and stir-fry for 2 minutes. Leave to cool.

4 Divide the mixture into 12 equal portions and place one portion on the edge of each spring roll wrapper. Fold in the sides and roll each one up, brushing the join with a little beaten egg to seal.

5 Deep-fry the spring rolls in batches in hot oil in a wok or large saucepan for 4–5 minutes, or until golden and crispy. Take care that the oil is not too hot or the spring rolls will brown on the outside before cooking on the inside. Remove and drain on paper towels. Keep each batch of spring rolls warm while the others are being cooked. Serve at once.

Step 2

Step 4

Step 5

Lettuce-Wrapped Minced (Ground) Meat

*Serve the minced (ground) meat and lettuce leaves on separate dishes:
the guests then wrap their own parcels.*

SERVES 4

INGREDIENTS

250 g/8 oz minced (ground) pork or chicken
1 tbsp finely chopped Chinese mushrooms
1 tbsp finely chopped water chestnuts
pinch of sugar
1 tsp light soy sauce
1 tsp Chinese rice wine or dry sherry
1 tsp cornflour (cornstarch)
2–3 tbsp vegetable oil
½ tsp finely chopped ginger root
1 tsp finely chopped spring onions (scallions)
1 tbsp finely chopped Szechuan
preserved vegetables (optional)
1 tbsp oyster sauce
a few drops of sesame oil
salt and pepper
8 crisp lettuce leaves, to serve

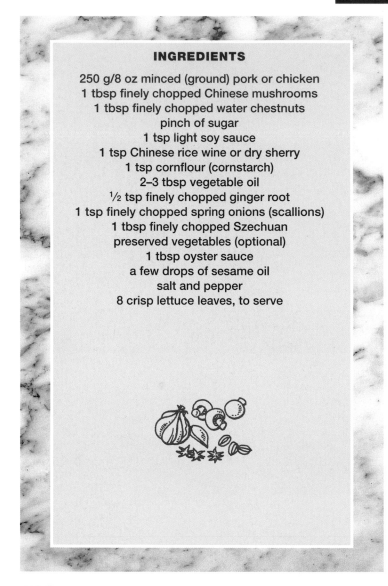

1 Mix the minced (ground) meat with the mushrooms, water chestnuts, sugar, soy sauce, wine, cornflour (cornstarch), and salt and pepper.

2 Heat the oil in a preheated wok or pan and add the ginger and spring onions (scallions) followed by the meat. Stir-fry for 1 minute.

3 Add the Szechuan preserved vegetables and continue stirring for 1 more minute. Add the oyster sauce and sesame oil, blend well and cook for 1 more minute. Remove to a warmed serving dish.

4 To serve: place about 2–3 tablespoons of the mixture on a lettuce leaf and roll it up tightly to form a small parcel. Eat with your fingers.

Step *1*

Step *2*

Step *3*

Deep-Fried Prawns (Shrimp)

Use raw tiger prawns (shrimp) in their shells. They are 7–10 cm/3–4
inches long, and you should get 18–20 prawns (shrimp) per 500 g/1 lb.

SERVES 4

INGREDIENTS

250–300 g/8–10 oz raw prawns
(shrimp) in their shells, defrosted if frozen
1 tbsp light soy sauce
1 tsp Chinese rice wine or dry sherry
2 tsp cornflour (cornstarch)
vegetable oil, for deep-frying
2–3 spring onions (scallions), to garnish

SPICY SALT AND PEPPER

1 tbsp salt
1 tsp ground Szechuan peppercorns
1 tsp five-spice powder

1 Pull the soft legs off the prawns (shrimp), but leave the body shell intact. Dry well on paper towels.

2 Place the prawns (shrimp) in a bowl with the soy sauce, wine and cornflour (cornstarch). Turn to coat and leave to marinate for about 25–30 minutes.

3 To make the spicy salt and pepper, mix the salt, pepper and five-spice powder together. Place in a dry frying pan (skillet) and stir-fry for about 3–4 minutes over a low heat, stirring constantly. Remove from the heat and allow to cool.

4 Heat the oil in a preheated wok until smoking, then deep-fry the prawns (shrimp) in batches until golden brown. Remove with a slotted spoon and drain thoroughly on paper towels.

5 Place the spring onions (scallions) in a bowl, pour on 1 tablespoon of the hot oil and leave for 30 seconds. Serve the prawns (shrimp) garnished with the spring onions (scallions), and with the spicy salt and pepper as a condiment.

Step *1*

Step *3*

Step *4*

Butterfly Prawns (Shrimp)

Use unpeeled, raw king or tiger prawns (shrimp)
which are about 7–10 cm (3–4 inches) long.

SERVES 4

INGREDIENTS

12 raw tiger prawns (shrimp) in their shells
2 tbsp light soy sauce
1 tbsp Chinese rice wine or dry sherry
1 tbsp cornflour (cornstarch)
2 eggs, lightly beaten
8–10 tbsp breadcrumbs
vegetable oil for deep-frying
salt and pepper
shredded lettuce leaves, to serve
chopped spring onions (scallions), to garnish

1 Shell and devein the prawns (shrimp) but leave the tails on. Split them in half from the underbelly about halfway along, leaving the tails still firmly attached.

2 Mix together the soy sauce, wine, cornflour (cornstarch), and salt and pepper in a bowl, add the prawns (shrimp) and turn to coat. Leave to marinate for 10–15 minutes.

3 Heat the oil in a preheated wok. Pick up each prawn (shrimp) by the tail, dip it in the beaten egg then roll it in the breadcrumbs to coat well.

4 Deep-fry the prawns (shrimp) in batches until golden brown. Remove them with a slotted spoon and drain on paper towels.

5 To serve, arrange the prawns (shrimp) neatly on a bed of lettuce leaves and garnish with spring onions (scallions), either raw or soaked in a tablespoon of the hot oil for about 30 seconds.

Step *1*

Step *3*

Step *3*

Deep-Fried Spare Ribs

The spare ribs should be chopped into small bite-sized pieces before or after cooking.

SERVES 4

INGREDIENTS

8–10 finger spare ribs
1 tsp five-spice powder or
1 tbsp mild curry powder
1 tbsp rice wine or dry sherry
1 egg
2 tbsp flour
vegetable oil for deep-frying
1 tsp finely shredded spring onions
(scallions)
1 tsp finely shredded fresh green or
red hot chillies, seeded
salt and pepper
Spicy Salt and Pepper (page 28), to serve

1 Chop the ribs into 3–4 small pieces. Place the ribs in a bowl with the five-spice or curry powder, wine, and salt and pepper. Turn to coat them then leave to marinate for 1–2 hours.

2 Mix the egg and flour together to make a batter. Dip the ribs in the batter one by one to coat well.

3 Heat the oil in a preheated wok until smoking. Deep-fry the ribs for 4–5 minutes, then remove with a slotted spoon and drain on paper towels.

4 Reheat the oil over a high heat and deep-fry the ribs once more for another minute. Remove and drain again on paper towels.

5 Pour 1 tablespoon of the hot oil over the spring onions (scallions) and chillies and leave for 30–40 seconds. Serve the ribs with spicy salt and pepper, garnished with the shredded spring onions (scallions) and chillies.

Step *1*

Step *2*

Step *3*

Pork with Chilli and Garlic Sauce

*Any leftovers from this dish can be used for a number of other dishes such
as Hot & Sour Soup (page 60), and Twice-Cooked Pork (page 158).*

SERVES 4

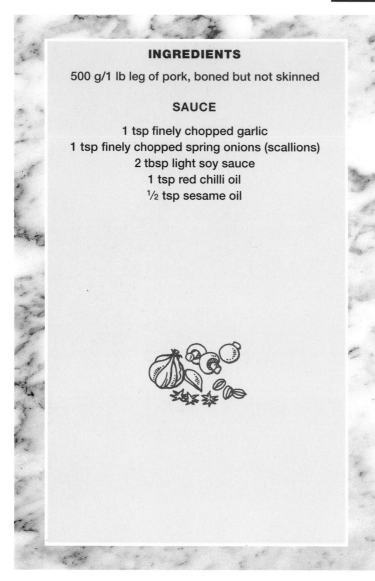

INGREDIENTS

500 g/1 lb leg of pork, boned but not skinned

SAUCE

1 tsp finely chopped garlic
1 tsp finely chopped spring onions (scallions)
2 tbsp light soy sauce
1 tsp red chilli oil
½ tsp sesame oil

1 Place the pork, tied together in one piece, in a large
pan, add enough cold water to cover, and bring to a
rolling boil over a medium heat.

2 Skim off the scum that rises to the surface, cover and
simmer gently for 25–30 minutes.

3 Leave the meat in the liquid to cool, under cover, for
at least 1–2 hours. Lift out the meat with 2 slotted
spoons and leave to cool completely, skin-side up, for 2–3
hours.

4 To serve, cut off the skin, leaving a very thin layer of
fat on top like a ham joint. Cut the meat in small thin
slices across the grain, and arrange neatly on a plate. Mix
together the sauce ingredients, and pour the sauce evenly
over the pork.

Step *2*

Step *3*

Step *4*

Barbecue Spare Ribs

This is a simplified version of the half saddle of pork ribs seen hanging in the windows of Cantonese restaurants. Use the specially small, thin ribs known as finger ribs.

SERVES 4

INGREDIENTS

500 g/1 lb finger spare ribs
1 tbsp sugar
1 tbsp light soy sauce
1 tbsp dark soy sauce
3 tbsp hoi-sin sauce
1 tbsp rice wine or dry sherry
4–5 tbsp water or Chinese Stock (page 16)
mild chilli sauce, to dip
coriander leaves, to garnish

1 Trim off any excess fat from the ribs and cut into pieces. Mix the ribs with the sugar, light and dark soy sauce, hoi-sin sauce and wine in a baking dish, and marinate for about 2–3 hours.

2 Add the water or stock to the ribs and spread them out in the dish. Roast in a preheated oven, 220°C/425°F/Gas Mark 7, for 15 minutes.

3 Turn the ribs over, lower the heat to 190°C/375°F/Gas Mark 5, and cook for 30–35 minutes longer.

4 To serve, chop each rib into 3–4 small, bite-sized pieces with a large knife or Chinese cleaver and arrange on a serving dish. Pour the sauce from the baking dish over them, garnish with coriander leaves, and serve with chilli sauce as a dip.

Step *2*

Step *3*

Step *4*

Barbecue Pork (Char Siu)

Also called honey-roasted pork, these are the strips of reddish meat sometimes seen hanging in the windows of Cantonese restaurants.

SERVES 4

INGREDIENTS

500 g/1 lb pork fillet
150 ml/¼ pint/⅔ cup boiling water
1 tbsp honey, dissolved with a little hot water
shredded lettuce, to serve

MARINADE

1 tbsp sugar
1 tbsp crushed yellow bean sauce
1 tbsp light soy sauce
1 tbsp hoi-sin sauce
1 tbsp oyster sauce
½ tsp chilli sauce
1 tbsp brandy or rum
1 tsp sesame oil

1 Cut the pork into strips about 2.5 cm/1 inch thick and 18–20 cm/7–8 inches long and place in a large shallow dish. Combine the marinade ingredients and add to the pork, turning until well coated. Cover, and leave to marinate for at least 3–4 hours, turning occasionally.

2 Remove the pork strips from the dish with a slotted spoon, reserving the marinade. Arrange the pork strips on a rack over a baking tin (pan). Place the tin (pan) in the preheated oven, 220°C/425°F/Gas Mark 7, and pour in the boiling water. Roast for about 10–15 minutes.

3 Lower the oven temperature to 180°C/350°F/Gas Mark 4. Baste the pork strips with the reserved marinade and turn. Roast for a further 10 minutes.

4 Remove the pork from the oven, brush with the honey syrup, and lightly brown under a medium hot grill (broiler) for 3–4 minutes, turning once or twice.

5 To serve, allow the pork to cool slightly before cutting it. Cut across the grain into thin slices and arrange on a bed of shredded lettuce. Make a sauce by boiling the marinade and the drippings in the baking tin (pan) for a few minutes, strain and pour over the pork.

Step *1*

Step *4*

Step *5*

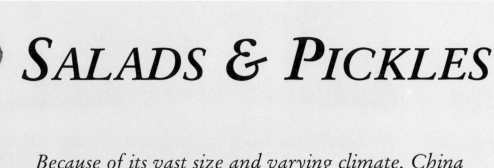

SALADS & PICKLES

Because of its vast size and varying climate, China produces an amazing variety of vegetables which play an important part in the diet. Although salads as we know them in the West do not feature greatly on the Chinese menu, many lightly cooked vegetable dishes can be classified as salads when allowed to cool and are lightly tossed with a dressing. Raw vegetables can be mixed in with cooked ones to provide contrasting texture.

Dressings provide the necessary note of sharpness and acidity and can be based on palate-tingling mixtures of lime, fish sauce, ginger, soy sauce and sesame oil, as well as the more familiar oil and vinegar.

For the Chinese, it is of the utmost importance to use the best, freshest vegetables available, preferably picked fresh as they are needed. Brief cooking and the necessary balance of texture and flavour, sweetness and acidity soon reveal inferior ingredients.

It is common practice in China to pickle vegetables for use in the winter months. These are used as a condiment, or stir-fried with vegetables or tofu (bean curd) or added to soups. You can also make pickles with briefly marinated vegetables such as Sweet and Sour Cucumber (page 44) to use as salads.

Sweet & Sour Tofu (Bean Curd) Salad

Tofu (bean curd) mixed with crisp stir-fried vegetables, then tossed in a piquant sweet and sour dressing makes an ideal light meal or starter.

SERVES 4–6

INGREDIENTS

2 tbsp vegetable oil
1 tbsp sesame oil
1 garlic clove, crushed
500 g/1 lb tofu (bean curd), cubed
1 onion, sliced
1 carrot, cut into julienne strips
1 stick celery, sliced
2 small red (bell) peppers,
cored, seeded and sliced
250 g/8 oz mangetout (snow peas),
trimmed and halved
125 g/4 oz broccoli,
trimmed and divided into florets
125g/4 oz thin French (green) beans, halved
2 tbsp oyster sauce
1 tbsp tamarind concentrate
1 tbsp fish sauce
1 tbsp tomato purée (paste)
1 tbsp light soy sauce
1 tbsp chilli sauce
2 tbsp sugar
1 tbsp white vinegar
pinch of ground star anise
1 tsp cornflour (cornstarch)
300 ml/½ pint/1¼ cups water

1 Heat the vegetable oil in a wok or large, heavy-based frying pan (skillet) until hot. Add the crushed garlic and cook for a few seconds.

2 Add the tofu (bean curd) in batches and stir-fry over a gentle heat, until golden on all sides. Remove with a slotted spoon and keep warm.

3 Add the onion, carrot, celery, red (bell) pepper, mangetout (snow peas), broccoli and green beans to the pan and stir-fry for about 2–3 minutes or until tender-crisp.

4 Add the oyster sauce, tamarind concentrate, fish sauce, tomato purée (paste), soy sauce, chilli sauce, sugar, vinegar and star anise, mixing well to blend. Stir-fry for a further 2 minutes.

5 Mix the cornflour (cornstarch) with the water and add to the pan with the fried tofu (bean curd). Stir-fry gently until the sauce boils and thickens slightly.

6 Serve the salad immediately, on warm plates.

Step *2*

Step *3*

Step *5*

Sweet & Sour Cucumber

*Chunks of cucumber are marinated in vinegar and sweetened
with honey to make a sweet and sour appetizer.*

SERVES 4

INGREDIENTS

1 cucumber
1 tsp salt
2 tsp honey
2 tbsp rice vinegar
3 tbsp chopped fresh coriander (cilantro)
2 tsp sesame oil
¼ tsp crushed red peppercorns
strips of red and yellow (bell) pepper, to garnish

1 Peel thin strips off the cucumber along the length. This gives a pretty striped effect. Cut the cucumber in quarters lengthways and then into 2.5 cm/1 inch long pieces. Place in a colander.

2 Sprinkle the salt over the cucumber and leave for 30 minutes to allow the salt to draw out excess water. Wash the cucumber thoroughly to remove the salt, drain and pat dry with paper towels.

3 Place the cucumber in a bowl. Combine the honey with the vinegar and pour over. Mix together and leave to marinate for 15 minutes.

4 Stir in the coriander (cilantro) and sesame oil, and place in a serving bowl.

5 Sprinkle over the crushed red peppercorns. Serve garnished with strips of red and yellow (bell) pepper.

Step *1*

Step *2*

Step *4*

Chinese Hot Salad

*Stir-fried vegetables with a little touch of chilli. To serve cold, add
French dressing as the vegetables cool, toss well and serve.*

SERVES 4

INGREDIENTS

1 tbsp dark soy sauce
1½–2 tsp bottled sweet chilli sauce
2 tbsp sherry
1 tbsp brown sugar
1 tbsp wine vinegar
2 tbsp sunflower oil
1 garlic clove, crushed
4 spring onions (scallions),
sliced thinly diagonally
250 g/8 oz courgettes (zucchini) cut into
julienne strips about 4 cm/1½ inches long
250 g/8 oz carrots, cut into julienne strips
about 4 cm/1½ inches long
1 red or green (bell) pepper,
cored, seeded and sliced thinly
400 g/14 oz can bean-sprouts, well drained
125 g/4 oz French (green) or fine beans,
cut into 5 cm/2 inch lengths
1 tbsp sesame oil
salt and pepper
1–2 tsp sesame seeds, to garnish

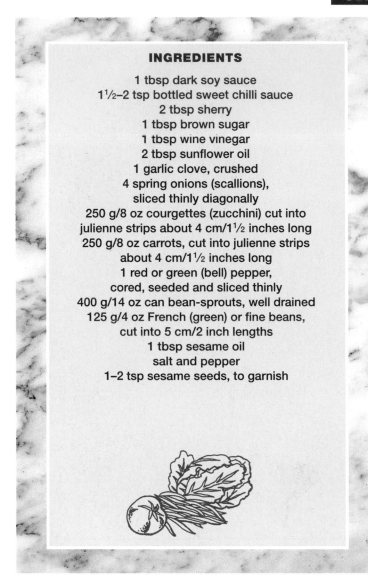

1 Blend the soy sauce, chilli sauce, sherry, sugar, vinegar, and salt and pepper together.

2 Heat the 2 tablespoons of sunflower oil in a wok, swirling it around until it is really hot.

3 Add the garlic and spring onions (scallions) to the wok and stir-fry for 1–2 minutes.

4 Add the courgettes (zucchini), carrots and (bell) pepper and stir-fry for 1–2 minutes, then add the soy sauce mixture and bring to the boil.

5 Add the bean-sprouts and French (green) beans and stir-fry for 1–2 minutes, making sure all the vegetables are thoroughly coated with the sauce.

6 Drizzle the sesame oil over the vegetables. Stir–fry for about 30 seconds and sprinkle with sesame seeds.

Step *1*

Step *4*

Step *5*

Oriental Salad

*This colourful crisp salad has a fresh orange dressing
and is topped with crunchy vermicelli.*

SERVES 4–6

INGREDIENTS

30 g/1 oz/¼ cup dried vermicelli
½ head Chinese leaves
125 g/4 oz/2 cups bean-sprouts
6 radishes
125 g/4 oz mangetout (snow peas)
1 large carrot
125 g/4 oz sprouting beans

DRESSING

juice of 1 orange
1 tbsp sesame seeds, toasted
1 tsp honey
1 tsp sesame oil
1 tbsp hazelnut oil

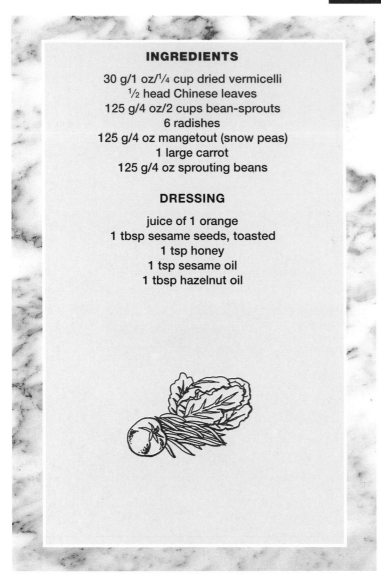

1 Break the vermicelli into small strands. Heat a wok or frying pan (skillet) and dry-fry the vermicelli until lightly golden. Remove from the pan and set aside.

2 Shred the Chinese leaves and wash with the bean-sprouts. Drain thoroughly and place in a large bowl. Slice the radishes. Trim the mangetout (snow peas) and cut each into 3. Cut the carrot into thin matchsticks. Add the sprouting beans and prepared vegetables to the bowl.

3 Place all the dressing ingredients in a screw-top jar and shake until well-blended. Pour over the salad and toss.

4 Transfer the salad to a serving bowl and sprinkle over the reserved vermicelli before serving.

Step *1*

Step *2*

Step *4*

Pickled Vegetables

Pickled vegetables can be marinated for as little as 30 minutes or for several days.

SERVES 4

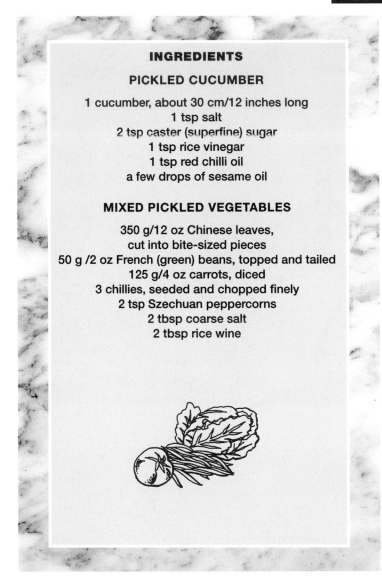

INGREDIENTS

PICKLED CUCUMBER

1 cucumber, about 30 cm/12 inches long
1 tsp salt
2 tsp caster (superfine) sugar
1 tsp rice vinegar
1 tsp red chilli oil
a few drops of sesame oil

MIXED PICKLED VEGETABLES

350 g/12 oz Chinese leaves,
cut into bite-sized pieces
50 g /2 oz French (green) beans, topped and tailed
125 g/4 oz carrots, diced
3 chillies, seeded and chopped finely
2 tsp Szechuan peppercorns
2 tbsp coarse salt
2 tbsp rice wine

PICKLED CUCUMBER

1 Halve the cucumber, unpeeled, lengthways. Scrape off the seeds and cut across into thick chunks.

2 Sprinkle with the salt and mix well. Leave to marinate for at least 20–30 minutes, longer if possible, then pour the juice away.

3 Mix the cucumber with the sugar, vinegar and chilli oil, and lightly sprinkle with the sesame oil just before serving.

MIXED PICKLED VEGETABLES

1 Place the vegetables in a glass bowl with the chillies, peppercorns, salt and wine. Stir well, cover and leave to marinate in the refrigerator for 4 days. Serve cold, as a salad.

Step *1*

Step *2*

Step *3*

Hot & Sour Duck Salad

This is a lovely tangy salad, drizzled with a lime juice and fish sauce dressing. It makes a splendid starter or light main course dish.

SERVES 4

INGREDIENTS

2 heads crisp salad lettuce,
washed and separated into leaves
2 shallots, sliced thinly
4 spring onions (scallions), chopped
1 celery stick, cut into julienne strips
5 cm/2 inch piece cucumber,
cut into julienne strips
125 g/4 oz/2 cups bean-sprouts
200 g/7 oz can water chestnuts,
drained and sliced
4 duck breast fillets, roasted and sliced
orange slices, to serve

DRESSING

3 tbsp fish sauce
1½ tbsp lime juice
2 garlic cloves, crushed
1 red chilli pepper, seeded and
chopped very finely
1 green chilli pepper, seeded and
chopped very finely
1 tsp palm sugar or demerara sugar

1 Mix the lettuce leaves with the shallots, spring onions (scallions), celery, cucumber, bean-sprouts and water chestnuts. Place the mixture on a large serving platter.

2 Arrange the duck breast slices on top of the salad in an attractive overlapping pattern.

3 To make the dressing, put the fish sauce, lime juice, garlic, chillies and sugar into a small pan. Heat gently, stirring constantly. Taste and adjust the piquancy if liked by adding more lime juice, or add more fish sauce to reduce the sharpness.

4 Drizzle the warm salad dressing over the duck salad and serve immediately.

Step *1*

Step *2*

Step *3*

SOUPS

Soup is not normally served as a separate course in China, except at formal occasions and banquets - and then it usually appears towards the end of the meal. At an everyday meal in Chinese homes it is quite common to have a large tureen of soup on the table which is served at the same time as the other dishes. The soup is almost always a clear broth in which a small amount of thinly sliced vegetables and/or meat have been quickly poached.

Although most Chinese soups are of the thin, clear variety, they do have a few thickened ones, such as Hot & Sour Soup (page 60) to which cornflour (cornstarch) is added. These soups can be eaten as a lunch or snack on their own.

The soup should ideally be made with a good stock. If this is unavailable, a Chinese cook would simply stir-fry the ingredients first in a little oil, then add water and seasonings (salt, soy sauce or monosodium glutamate) to make an instant soup fit for the gods! If you use a stock cube, remember to reduce the amount of seasonings in the recipe as most commercially made bouillon cubes are fairly salty. It is always worth making your own Chinese stock (page 16) if you have time.

Mushroom & Cucumber Noodle Soup

A light, refreshing clear soup of mushrooms, cucumber and small pieces of rice noodles, flavoured with soy sauce and a touch of garlic.

SERVES 4

INGREDIENTS

125 g/4 oz flat or open-cup mushrooms
½ cucumber
2 spring onions (scallions)
1 garlic clove
2 tbsp vegetable oil
30 g/1 oz/¼ cup Chinese rice noodles
¾ tsp salt
1 tbsp soy sauce

1 Wash the mushrooms and slice thinly. Do not remove the peel as this adds more flavour. Halve the cucumber lengthways. Scoop out the seeds, using a teaspoon, and slice the cucumber thinly.

2 Chop the spring onions (scallions) finely and cut the garlic clove into thin strips.

3 Heat the oil in a wok or large saucepan. Add the spring onions (scallions) and garlic, and stir-fry for 30 seconds. Add the mushrooms and stir-fry for 2–3 minutes.

4 Stir in 600 ml/1 pint/2½ cups water. Break the noodles into short lengths and add them to the soup. Bring to the boil.

5 Add the cucumber slices, salt and soy sauce, and simmer for 2–3 minutes.

6 Serve the soup in warmed bowls, distributing the noodles and vegetables evenly.

Step *1*

Step *3*

Step *5*

Mixed Vegetable Soup

Select three or four vegetables for this soup: the Chinese like to blend different colours, flavours and textures to create harmony as well as contrast.

SERVES 4

INGREDIENTS

about 30–60 g/1–2 oz each of 3 or 4
of the following:
mushrooms, carrots,
asparagus, mangetout (snow peas),
bamboo shoots, baby sweetcorn,
cucumber, tomatoes,
spinach, lettuce,
Chinese leaves, tofu (bean curd)
600 ml/1 pint/2 ½ cups Chinese Stock (page 16)
1 tbsp light soy sauce
a few drops of sesame oil (optional)
salt and pepper
finely chopped spring onions (scallions),
to garnish

1 Cut your selection of vegetables into roughly uniform shapes and sizes (slices, shreds or cubes).

2 Bring the stock to a rolling boil in a wok and add the vegetables, bearing in mind that some require a longer cooking time than others: add carrots and baby sweetcorn first, cook for 2 minutes, then add asparagus, mushrooms, Chinese leaves, bean curd, and cook for another minute.

3 Add the spinach, lettuce, watercress, cucumber and tomato. Stir, and bring the soup back to the boil.

4 Add soy sauce and the sesame oil, and adjust the seasoning. Serve hot, garnished with spring onions (scallions).

Step *1*

Step *3*

Step *4*

Hot & Sour Soup

This is the favourite soup in Chinese restaurants throughout the world.

SERVES 4

INGREDIENTS

4–6 dried Chinese mushrooms, soaked
in warm water for 30 minutes
125 g/4 oz cooked pork or chicken
1 cake tofu (bean curd)
60 g/2 oz canned sliced bamboo shoots, drained
600 ml/1 pint/2½ cups Chinese Stock (page 16)
or water
1 tbsp Chinese rice wine or dry sherry
1 tbsp light soy sauce
2 tbsp rice vinegar
1 tbsp Cornflour (Cornstarch) Paste (page 16)
salt and pepper
2–3 spring onions (scallions),
sliced thinly, to serve

1 Drain the mushrooms, squeeze dry and discard the hard stalks. Thinly slice the mushrooms.

2 Thinly slice the meat, tofu (bean curd) and bamboo shoots into narrow shreds.

3 Bring the stock or water to a rolling boil in a wok or large pan and add all the ingredients. Bring back to the boil then simmer for about 1 minute.

4 Add the wine, soy sauce, vinegar, and salt and pepper.

5 Bring back to the boil once more, stirring in the cornflour (cornstarch) paste to thicken the soup. Serve hot, sprinkled with the spring onions (scallions).

Step *1*

Step *2*

Step *5*

Vegetarian Hot & Sour Soup

This is a popular Chinese soup, which is unusual in that it is thickened.
The 'hot' flavour is achieved by the addition of plenty of black pepper.

SERVES 4

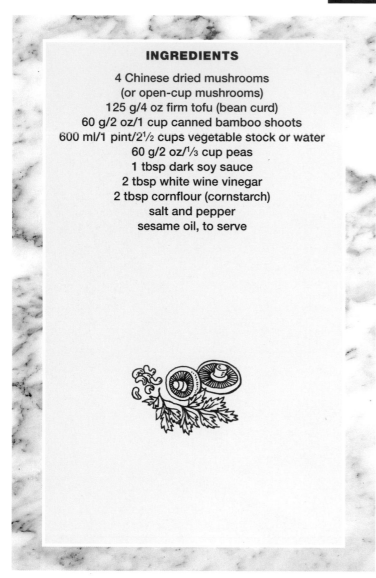

INGREDIENTS

4 Chinese dried mushrooms
(or open-cup mushrooms)
125 g/4 oz firm tofu (bean curd)
60 g/2 oz/1 cup canned bamboo shoots
600 ml/1 pint/2½ cups vegetable stock or water
60 g/2 oz/⅓ cup peas
1 tbsp dark soy sauce
2 tbsp white wine vinegar
2 tbsp cornflour (cornstarch)
salt and pepper
sesame oil, to serve

1 Place the dried mushrooms in a bowl and cover with warm water. Leave to soak for 20–25 minutes.

2 Drain the mushrooms and squeeze out the excess water, reserving this. Remove the tough centres and cut the mushrooms into thin shreds. Shred the tofu (bean curd) and bamboo shoots.

3 Bring the stock or water to the boil in a large saucepan. Add the mushrooms, tofu (bean curd), bamboo shoots and peas. Simmer for 2 minutes.

4 Mix together the soy sauce, vinegar and cornflour (cornstarch) with 2 tablespoons of the reserved mushroom liquid. Stir into the soup with the remaining mushroom liquid. Bring to the boil and season with salt and plenty of pepper. Simmer for 2 minutes.

5 Serve in warmed bowls with a few drops of sesame oil in each.

Step *2*

Step *3*

Step *4*

Wonton Soup

Filled wontons are served in a clear soup. The recipe for the wonton skins makes 24 but the soup requires only 12 – freeze the rest for another time.

SERVES 4

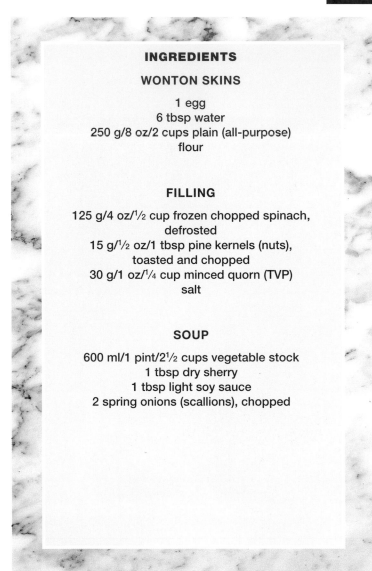

INGREDIENTS

WONTON SKINS

1 egg
6 tbsp water
250 g/8 oz/2 cups plain (all-purpose) flour

FILLING

125 g/4 oz/½ cup frozen chopped spinach, defrosted
15 g/½ oz/1 tbsp pine kernels (nuts), toasted and chopped
30 g/1 oz/¼ cup minced quorn (TVP)
salt

SOUP

600 ml/1 pint/2½ cups vegetable stock
1 tbsp dry sherry
1 tbsp light soy sauce
2 spring onions (scallions), chopped

1 Beat the egg lightly in a bowl and mix with the water. Stir in the flour to form a stiff dough. Knead lightly, then cover with a damp cloth and leave to rest for 30 minutes.

2 Roll the dough out into a large sheet about 1.5 mm/¼ inch thick. Cut out 24 × 7 cm/3 inch squares. Dust each one lightly with flour. Only 12 squares are required for the soup so freeze the remainder.

3 To make the filling, squeeze out the excess water from the spinach. Mix the spinach with the pine kernels (nuts) and quorn (TVP). Season with salt.

4 Divide the mixture into 12 equal portions and place one portion in the centre of each square. Seal by bringing the opposite corners of each square together and squeezing well.

5 To make the soup, bring the stock, sherry and soy sauce to the boil, add the wontons and boil rapidly for 2–3 minutes. Add the spring onions (scallions) and serve in warmed bowls immediately

Step *2*

Step *4*

Step *5*

Spinach & Tofu (Bean Curd) Soup

This is a very colourful and delicious soup. If spinach is not in season,
watercress or lettuce can be used instead.

SERVES 4

INGREDIENTS

1 cake tofu (bean curd)
125 g/4 oz spinach leaves without stems
750 ml/1¼ pints/3 cups Chinese Stock (page 16)
or water
1 tbsp light soy sauce
salt and pepper

1 Cut the tofu (bean curd) into small pieces about 5 mm (¼ inch) thick. Wash the spinach leaves and cut them into small pieces or shreds, discarding any discoloured leaves and tough stalks. (If possible, use fresh young spinach leaves, which have not yet developed tough ribs. Otherwise, it is important to cut out all the ribs and stems for this soup.)

2 In a wok or large pan, bring the stock to a rolling boil. Add the tofu (bean curd) and soy sauce, bring back to the boil and simmer for about 2 minutes over a medium heat.

3 Add the spinach and simmer for 1 more minute.

4 Skim the surface of the soup to make it clear, adjust the seasoning and serve.

Step *1*

Step *2*

Step *3*

Seafood & Tofu (Bean Curd) Soup

Use prawn (shrimp), squid or scallops,
or a combination of all three.

SERVES 4

INGREDIENTS

250 g/8 oz seafood, such as peeled prawns
(shrimp), squid, scallops, defrosted if frozen
½ egg white, beaten lightly
1 tbsp Cornflour (Cornstarch) Paste (page 16)
1 cake tofu (bean curd)
750 ml/1¼ pints/3 cups Chinese Stock (page 16)
1 tbsp light soy sauce
salt and pepper
fresh coriander (cilantro) leaves, to garnish (optional)

1 Small prawns (shrimp) can be left whole; larger ones should be cut into smaller pieces. Cut the squid and scallops into small pieces.

2 If raw, mix the prawns (shrimp) and scallops with the egg white and cornflour (cornstarch) paste to prevent them from becoming tough when they are cooked.

3 Cut the tofu (bean curd) into about 24 small cubes.

4 Bring the stock to a rolling boil. Add the tofu (bean curd) and soy sauce, bring back to the boil and simmer for 1 minute.

5 Stir in the seafood, raw pieces first, pre-cooked ones last. Bring back to boil and simmer for just 1 minute. Adjust the seasoning and serve garnished with coriander (cilantro) leaves, if liked.

Step *1*

Step *2*

Step *5*

Fish & Vegetable Soup

A chunky fish soup with strips of vegetables,
flavoured with ginger and lemon, makes a meal in itself.

SERVES 4

INGREDIENTS

250 g/8 oz white fish fillets, such as
cod, halibut, haddock, sole
½ tsp ground ginger
½ tsp salt
1 small leek, trimmed and sliced
1 tbsp sunflower oil
1 large carrot, cut into julienne strips
8 canned water chestnuts, sliced thinly
1.25 litres/2 pints/5 cups fish or vegetable stock
1 tbsp lemon juice
1 tbsp light soy sauce
1 large courgette (zucchini),
cut into julienne strips
2–4 crab sticks (optional), defrosted if frozen
pepper

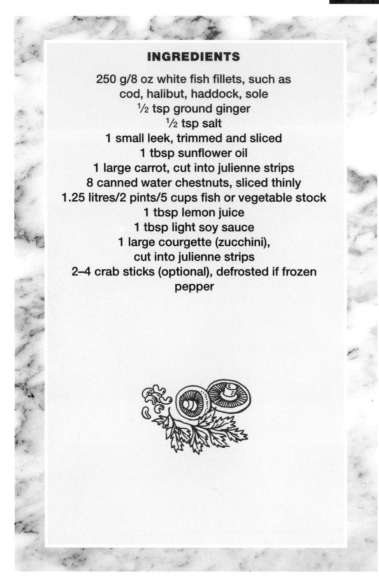

1 Remove any skin from the fish and cut the fish into cubes, about 2.5 cm/1 inch. Combine the ground ginger and salt and rub into the fish. Leave to marinate for at least 30 minutes.

2 Meanwhile, divide the green and white parts of the leek. Cut each part into 2.5 cm/1 inch lengths and then into julienne strips down the length of each piece, keeping the two parts separate. Slice the crab sticks into 1 cm/½ inch pieces.

3 Heat the oil in the wok, swirling it around so it is really hot. Add the white part of the leek and stir-fry for a couple of minutes, then add the carrots and water chestnuts and continue to cook for 1–2 minutes, stirring thoroughly.

4 Add the stock and bring to the boil, then add the lemon juice and soy sauce and simmer for 2 minutes.

5 Add the fish and continue to cook for about 5 minutes until the fish begins to break up a little, then add the green part of the leek and the courgettes (zucchini) and simmer for about 1 minute. Add the sliced crab sticks, if using, and season to taste with pepper. Simmer for a further minute or so and serve piping hot.

Step *1*

Step *2*

Step *5*

Three-Flavour Soup

*Ideally, use raw prawns (shrimp) in this soup. If that is not possible,
add ready-cooked ones at the very last stage.*

SERVES 4

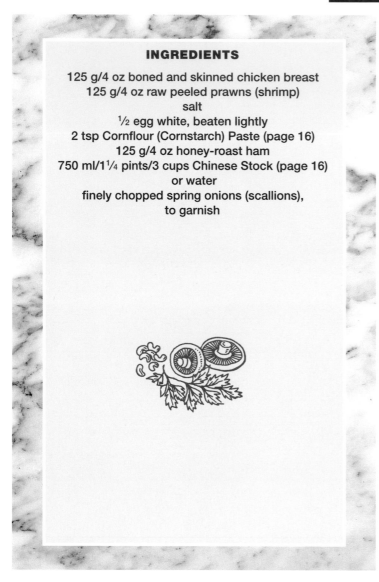

INGREDIENTS

125 g/4 oz boned and skinned chicken breast
125 g/4 oz raw peeled prawns (shrimp)
salt
½ egg white, beaten lightly
2 tsp Cornflour (Cornstarch) Paste (page 16)
125 g/4 oz honey-roast ham
750 ml/1¼ pints/3 cups Chinese Stock (page 16)
or water
finely chopped spring onions (scallions),
to garnish

1 Thinly slice the chicken into small shreds. If the
prawns (shrimp) are large, cut each in half
lengthways, otherwise leave whole.

2 Place the chicken and prawns (shrimps) in a bowl and
mix with a pinch of salt, the egg white and cornflour
(cornstarch) paste until well coated.

3 Cut the ham into small thin slices roughly the same
size as the chicken pieces.

4 Bring the stock or water to a rolling boil, add the
chicken, the raw prawns (shrimps) and the ham.
Bring the soup back to the boil, and simmer for 1 minute.

5 Adjust the seasoning and serve the soup hot,
garnished with the spring onions (scallions).

Step *2*

Step *3*

Step *4*

Prawn (Shrimp) Soup

A mixture of textures and flavours make this an interesting and colourful soup. The egg may be made into a flat omelette and added as thin strips.

SERVES 4

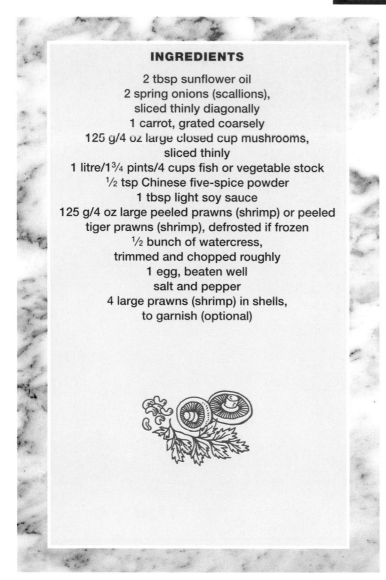

INGREDIENTS

2 tbsp sunflower oil
2 spring onions (scallions),
sliced thinly diagonally
1 carrot, grated coarsely
125 g/4 oz large closed cup mushrooms,
sliced thinly
1 litre/1¾ pints/4 cups fish or vegetable stock
½ tsp Chinese five-spice powder
1 tbsp light soy sauce
125 g/4 oz large peeled prawns (shrimp) or peeled
tiger prawns (shrimp), defrosted if frozen
½ bunch of watercress,
trimmed and chopped roughly
1 egg, beaten well
salt and pepper
4 large prawns (shrimp) in shells,
to garnish (optional)

1 Heat the oil in a wok, swirling it around until really hot. Add the spring onions (scallions) and stir-fry for a minute then add the carrots and mushrooms and continue to cook for about 2 minutes.

2 Add the stock and bring up to the boil then season to taste with salt and pepper, five-spice powder and soy sauce. Simmer for 5 minutes.

3 If the prawns (shrimp) are really large, cut them in half before adding to the wok, then continue to simmer for 3–4 minutes.

4 Add the roughly chopped watercress to the wok and mix well, then slowly pour in the beaten egg in a circular movement so that it cooks in threads in the soup.

5 Adjust the seasoning and serve each portion topped with a whole prawn (shrimp).

Step *1*

Step *2*

Step *4*

Sweetcorn & Crab Meat Soup

You must use American-style creamed sweetcorn for this soup since it originated in the USA! Chicken can be used instead of the crab meat.

SERVES 4

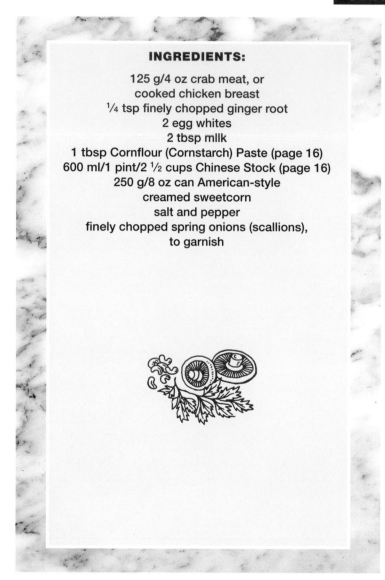

INGREDIENTS:

125 g/4 oz crab meat, or
cooked chicken breast
¼ tsp finely chopped ginger root
2 egg whites
2 tbsp mllk
1 tbsp Cornflour (Cornstarch) Paste (page 16)
600 ml/1 pint/2 ½ cups Chinese Stock (page 16)
250 g/8 oz can American-style
creamed sweetcorn
salt and pepper
finely chopped spring onions (scallions),
to garnish

1 Flake the crab meat (or coarsely chop the chicken breast) and mix with the ginger.

2 Beat the egg whites until frothy, add the milk and cornflour (cornstarch) paste and beat again until smooth. Blend in the crab or chicken.

3 In a wok or large frying pan (skillet), bring the stock to the boil, add the creamed sweetcorn and bring back to the boil.

4 Stir in the crab meat or chicken pieces and egg-white mixture, adjust the seasoning and stir gently until the mixture is well blended. Serve hot, garnished with chopped spring onions (scallions).

Step *2*

Step *3*

Step *4*

Chicken & Sweetcorn Soup

A hint of chilli and sherry flavour this chicken and sweetcorn soup which contains red (bell) pepper and tomato for colour and flavour.

SERVES 4

INGREDIENTS

1 boned and skinned chicken breast,
about 175 g/6 oz
2 tbsp sunflower oil
2–3 spring onions (scallions),
thinly sliced diagonally
1 small or ½ large red (bell) pepper,
cored, seeded and sliced thinly
1 garlic clove, crushed
125 g/4 oz baby sweetcorn, sliced thinly
1 litre/1¾ pints/4 cups chicken stock
200 g/7 oz can sweetcorn niblets,
well drained
2 tbsp sherry
2–3 tsp bottled sweet chilli sauce
2–3 tsp cornflour (cornstarch)
2 tomatoes, peeled, quartered and seeded,
then sliced
salt and pepper
freshly chopped coriander (cilantro)
or parsley, to garnish

1 Cut the chicken breast into 4 strips lengthways, then cut each strip into narrow slices across the grain.

2 Heat the oil in a wok, swirling it around until it is really hot. Add the chicken and stir-fry for 3–4 minutes, spreading it out over the wok until it is well sealed all over and almost cooked.

3 Add the spring onions (scallions), (bell) pepper and garlic and continue to stir-fry for 2–3 minutes, then add the baby sweetcorn and stock and bring to the boil.

4 Add the corn niblets, sherry and sweet chilli sauce and salt to taste and simmer for 5 minutes, stirring from time to time.

5 Blend the cornflour (cornstarch) with a little cold water, add to the soup and bring to the boil. Add the strips of tomato, adjust the seasoning and simmer for a few minutes. Serve the soup very hot, sprinkled with finely chopped coriander (cilantro) or parsley.

Step *2*

Step *3*

Step *4*

Chicken Soup with Almonds

This soup can also be made using turkey or pheasant breasts.
Pheasant gives a stronger, gamey flavour.

SERVES 4

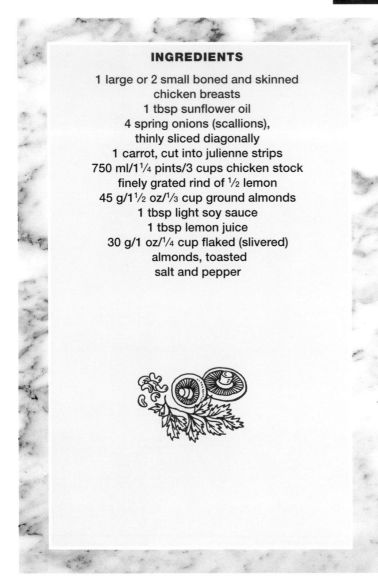

INGREDIENTS

1 large or 2 small boned and skinned
chicken breasts
1 tbsp sunflower oil
4 spring onions (scallions),
thinly sliced diagonally
1 carrot, cut into julienne strips
750 ml/1¼ pints/3 cups chicken stock
finely grated rind of ½ lemon
45 g/1½ oz/⅓ cup ground almonds
1 tbsp light soy sauce
1 tbsp lemon juice
30 g/1 oz/¼ cup flaked (slivered)
almonds, toasted
salt and pepper

1 Cut each breast into 4 strips lengthways, then slice very thinly across the grain to give shreds of chicken.

2 Heat the oil in the wok, swirling it around until really hot. Add the chicken and toss for 3–4 minutes until sealed and almost cooked through. Then add the carrot and continue to cook for 2–3 minutes, stirring all the time. Add the spring onions (scallions) and stir.

3 Add the stock to the wok and bring to the boil. Add the lemon rind, ground almonds, soy sauce, lemon juice and plenty of seasoning. Bring back to the boil and simmer, uncovered, for 5 minutes, stirring occasionally.

4 Add most of the toasted flaked (slivered) almonds and continue to cook for a further 1–2 minutes. Check the seasoning.

5 Serve the soup very hot, in individual bowls, sprinkled with the remaining almonds.

Step *1*

Step *2*

Step *3*

Noodles in Soup

Noodles in soup (tang mein) are more popular than fried noodles (chow mein)
in China. You can use different ingredients for the dressing if preferred.

SERVES 4

INGREDIENTS

250 g/8 oz chicken fillet, pork fillet,
or any other cooked meat
3–4 Chinese dried mushrooms, soaked
in warm water for 30 minutes
125 g/4 oz canned sliced bamboo shoots,
rinsed and drained
125 g/4 oz spinach leaves, lettuce hearts,
or Chinese leaves, shredded
2 spring onions (scallions), shredded finely
250 g/8 oz egg noodles
about 600 ml/1 pint/2½ cups Chinese Stock (page 16)
2 tbsp light soy sauce
2 tbsp vegetable oil
1 tsp salt
½ tsp sugar
2 tsp Chinese rice wine or dry sherry
a few drops of sesame oil
1 tsp red chilli oil (optional)

1 Cut the meat into thin shreds. Squeeze dry the soaked mushrooms and discard the hard stalk.

2 Thinly shred the mushrooms, bamboo shoots, spinach leaves and spring onions (scallions).

3 Cook the noodles in boiling water according to the instructions on the packet, then drain and rinse under cold water. Place in a bowl. Bring the stock to a boil, add about 1 tablespoon soy sauce and pour over the noodles. Keep warm.

4 Heat the oil in a pre-heated wok, add the meat, vegetables and about half of the spring onions (scallions). Stir-fry for about 2–3 minutes. Add the salt, sugar, wine, sesame oil and chilli oil, if using.

5 Pour the mixture in the wok over the noodles, garnish with the remaining spring onions (scallions) and serve immediately.

Step *2*

Step *4*

Step *5*

Pork & Szechuan Vegetable Soup

*Sold in cans, Szechuan preserved vegetable is pickled mustard root which
is quite hot and salty, so rinse in water before use.*

SERVES 4

INGREDIENTS

250 g/8 oz pork fillet
2 tsp Cornflour (Cornstarch) Paste (page 16)
125 g/4 oz Szechuan preserved vegetable
750 ml/1¼ pints/3 cups Chinese Stock (page 16)
or water
salt and pepper
a few drops of sesame oil (optional)
2–3 spring onions (scallions), sliced,
to garnish

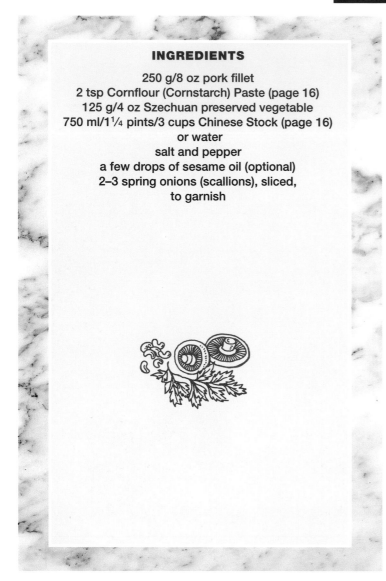

1 Cut the pork across the grain into thin shreds and mix with the cornflour (cornstarch) paste.

2 Wash and rinse the Szechuan preserved vegetable, then cut into thin shreds the same size as the pork.

3 Bring the stock or water to a rolling boil, add the pork and stir to separate the shreds. Bring back to the boil.

4 Add the Szechuan preserved vegetable and bring back to the boil once more. Adjust the seasoning and sprinkle with sesame oil. Serve hot, garnished with spring onions (scallions).

Step *1*

Step *2*

Step *3*

FISH & SEAFOOD

China's many miles of coastline, rivers and lakes offer an enormous variety of fresh and salt-water fish and seafood. Among the most popular varieties are carp, bass, bream, Mandarin fish (a type of perch), shad, grouper and sole. Seafood such as clams, crab, crawfish, prawns (shrimp) and lobsters are also widely eaten and freshwater crabs with their soft shells, are considered a great delicacy. Dishes which include shark's fins, abalone, squid and edible seaweed are also common. Although fish and seafood are widely eaten in China, the Chinese do not like fishy smells. Ginger, garlic, and salty black bean sauce are often used to disguise such smells. Favourite cooking methods are steaming, and quick poaching in boiling water or broth. Lobster and crabs are sometimes fried at very high temperatures in a flavoured oil which penetrates the cracked shells and creates the most delectable sauce which the Chinese love to suck from the shells. The process of buying and cooking fish is taken very seriously in China, as it is a highly esteemed food. No cook with any pride would dream of buying anything but a live fish, which are purchased in leakproof water-filled baskets and kept alive until just before cooking.

Stir-Fried Prawns (Shrimp) & Vegetables

This colourful and delicious dish is cooked with vegetables.
Vary them according to seasonal availability.

SERVES 4

INGREDIENTS

60 g/2 oz mangetout (snow peas)
½ small carrot, sliced thinly lengthways
60 g/2 oz baby sweetcorn
60 g/2 oz straw mushrooms
175–250 g/6–8 oz raw tiger prawns (shrimp), peeled
1 tsp salt
½ egg white, beaten lightly
1 tsp Cornflour (Cornstarch) Paste (page 16)
about 300ml/½ pint/1¼ cups vegetable oil
1 spring onion (scallion), cut into short sections
4 slices ginger root, chopped finely
½ tsp sugar
1 tbsp light soy sauce
1 tsp Chinese rice wine or dry sherry
a few drops of sesame oil

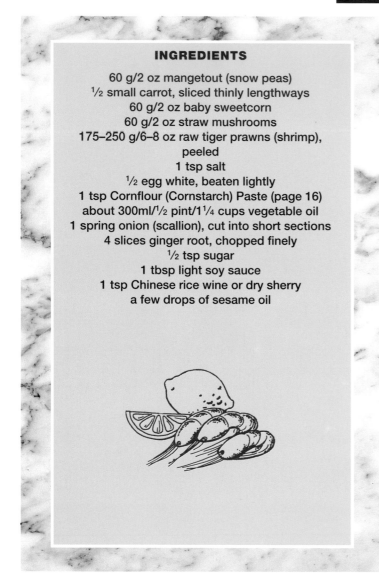

1 Top and tail the mangetout (snow peas). Cut the carrot into the same size as the mangetout (snow peas). Halve the baby sweetcorn and straw mushrooms.

2 Mix the prawns (shrimp) with a pinch of the salt, the egg white and cornflour (cornstarch) paste.

3 Heat a wok over high heat for 2–3 minutes, then add the oil and heat to medium-hot. Add the prawns (shrimp), stirring to separate them. Remove with a slotted spoon as soon as the colour changes.

4 Pour off the oil, leaving about 1 tablespoon in the wok. Add the mangetout (snow peas), carrot, sweetcorn, mushrooms, spring onion (scallion) and ginger root. Stir-fry for about 1 minute.

5 Add the prawns (shrimp) and the sugar, soy sauce and rice wine. Blend well. Sprinkle with the sesame oil and serve hot.

Step *1*

Step *3*

Step *5*

Stir-Fried Prawns (Shrimp)

The green (bell) peppers in this dish can be replaced by either mangetout (snow peas), or broccoli.

SERVES 4

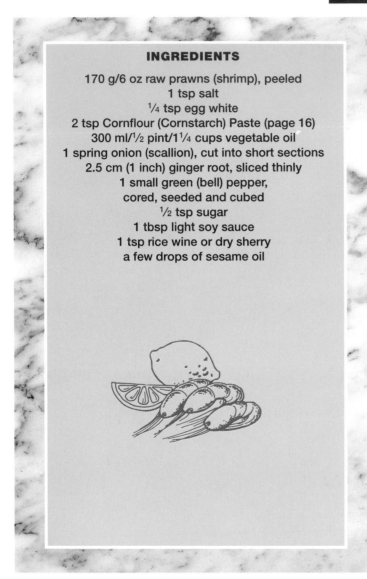

INGREDIENTS

170 g/6 oz raw prawns (shrimp), peeled
1 tsp salt
¼ tsp egg white
2 tsp Cornflour (Cornstarch) Paste (page 16)
300 ml/½ pint/1¼ cups vegetable oil
1 spring onion (scallion), cut into short sections
2.5 cm (1 inch) ginger root, sliced thinly
1 small green (bell) pepper,
cored, seeded and cubed
½ tsp sugar
1 tbsp light soy sauce
1 tsp rice wine or dry sherry
a few drops of sesame oil

1 Mix the prawns (shrimp) with a pinch of the salt, the egg white and cornflour (cornstarch) paste until they are all well coated.

2 Heat the oil in a preheated wok and stir-fry the prawns (shrimp) for 30–40 seconds only. Remove and drain on paper towels.

3 Pour off the oil, leaving about 1 tablespoon in the wok. Add the spring onion (scallion) and ginger to flavour the oil for a few seconds, then add the green (bell) pepper and stir-fry for about 1 minute.

4 Add the remaining salt and the sugar followed by the prawns (shrimp). Continue stirring for another minute or so, then add the soy sauce and wine and blend well. Sprinkle with sesame oil and serve immediately.

Step *2*

Step *3*

Step *4*

Szechuan Prawns (Shrimp)

Use raw prawns (shrimp) if possible, otherwise omit steps 1
and 2 and add the cooked prawns (shrimp) before the sauce at step 3.

SERVES 4

INGREDIENTS

250–300 g/8–10 oz raw tiger prawns (shrimp)
pinch of salt
½ egg white, lightly beaten
1 tsp Cornflour (Cornstarch) Paste (page 16)
600 ml/1 pint/2½ cups vegetable oil
fresh coriander (cilantro) leaves, to garnish

SAUCE

1 tsp finely chopped ginger root
2 spring onions (scallions), chopped finely
1 garlic clove, chopped finely
3–4 small dried red chillies, seeded and chopped
1 tbsp light soy sauce
1 tsp rice wine or dry sherry
1 tbsp tomato purée (paste)
1 tbsp oyster sauce
2–3 tbsp Chinese Stock (page 16) or water
a few drops of sesame oil

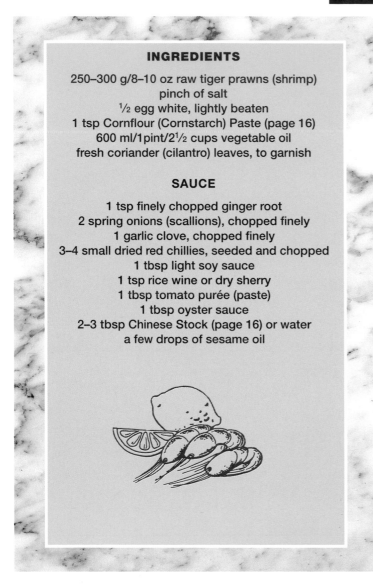

1 Peel the raw prawns (shrimp), then mix with the salt, egg white and cornflour (cornstarch) paste until well coated.

2 Heat the oil in a preheated wok until it is smoking, then deep-fry the prawns (shrimp) in hot oil for about 1 minute. Remove with a slotted spoon and drain on paper towels.

3 Pour off the oil, leaving about 1 tablespoon in the wok. Add all the ingredients for the sauce, bring to the boil and stir until smooth and well blended.

4 Add the prawns (shrimp) to the sauce, stirring to blend. Garnish with coriander (cilantro) leaves.

Step *1*

Step *3*

Step *4*

Sizzled Chilli Prawns (Shrimp)

*Large prawns (shrimp) are marinated in a chilli mixture then
stir-fried with cashews. Serve with fluffy rice and braised vegetables.*

SERVES 4

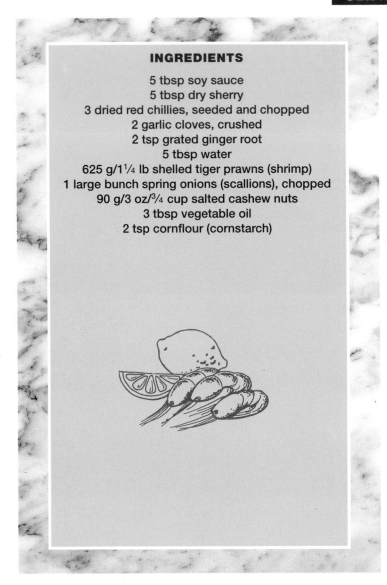

INGREDIENTS

5 tbsp soy sauce
5 tbsp dry sherry
3 dried red chillies, seeded and chopped
2 garlic cloves, crushed
2 tsp grated ginger root
5 tbsp water
625 g/1¼ lb shelled tiger prawns (shrimp)
1 large bunch spring onions (scallions), chopped
90 g/3 oz/¾ cup salted cashew nuts
3 tbsp vegetable oil
2 tsp cornflour (cornstarch)

1 Mix the soy sauce with the sherry, chillies, garlic, ginger and water in a large bowl.

2 Add the prawns (shrimp), spring onions (scallions) and cashews and mix well. Cover tightly and leave to marinate for at least 2 hours, stirring occasionally.

3 Heat the oil in a large, heavy-based frying pan (skillet) or wok. Remove the prawns (shrimp), spring onions (scallions) and cashews from the marinade with a slotted spoon and add to the pan, reserving the marinade. Stir-fry over a high heat for 1–2 minutes.

4 Mix the reserved marinade with the cornflour (cornstarch). Add to the pan and stir-fry for about 30 seconds, until the marinade forms a slightly thickened shiny glaze over the prawn (shrimp) mixture.

5 Serve immediately, with rice and braised vegetables.

Step *1*

Step *2*

Step *3*

Prawn (Shrimp) Stir-Fry with Lemon Grass

*A very quick and tasty stir-fry using prawns (shrimp),
cucumber and oyster mushrooms, flavoured with lemon grass.*

SERVES 4

INGREDIENTS

½ cucumber
2 tsp cornflour (cornstarch)
2 tbsp water
1 tbsp dark soy sauce
½ tsp fish sauce
2 tbsp sunflower oil
6 spring onions (scallions),
halved lengthways
and cut into 4 cm/1½ inch lengths
1 stalk lemon grass, sliced thinly
1 garlic clove, chopped
1 tsp chopped fresh red chilli
125 g/4 oz oyster mushrooms
1 tsp chopped ginger root
350 g/12 oz cooked peeled prawns (shrimp)
2 tbsp dry sherry or rice wine
boiled rice, to serve

1 Cut the cucumber into thin strips measuring about 5 mm x 4 cm/¼ x 1¾ inches.

2 Mix together the cornflour (cornstarch), water, soy sauce and fish sauce until smooth and set aside.

3 Heat the oil in a wok or large frying pan (skillet), add the spring onions (scallions), cucumber, lemon grass, garlic, chilli, mushrooms and ginger, and stir-fry for 2 minutes.

4 Add the prawns (shrimp) and stir-fry for a further minute.

5 Stir the cornflour (cornstarch) mixture and dry sherry or rice wine into the pan and heat through, stirring, until the sauce has thickened. Serve immediately with boiled rice.

Step *1*

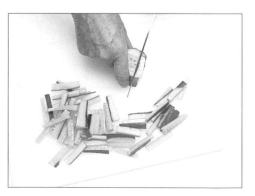

Step *3*

Step *5*

Sweet & Sour Prawns (Shrimp) with Chilli

Use raw prawns (shrimp) if possible.
Omit steps 1 and 2 if ready-cooked ones are used.

SERVES 4

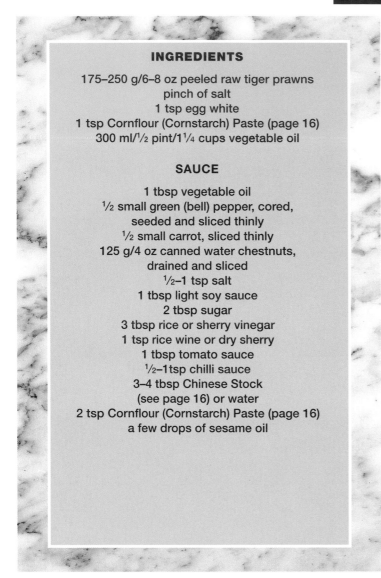

INGREDIENTS

175–250 g/6–8 oz peeled raw tiger prawns
pinch of salt
1 tsp egg white
1 tsp Cornflour (Cornstarch) Paste (page 16)
300 ml/½ pint/1¼ cups vegetable oil

SAUCE

1 tbsp vegetable oil
½ small green (bell) pepper, cored,
seeded and sliced thinly
½ small carrot, sliced thinly
125 g/4 oz canned water chestnuts,
drained and sliced
½–1 tsp salt
1 tbsp light soy sauce
2 tbsp sugar
3 tbsp rice or sherry vinegar
1 tsp rice wine or dry sherry
1 tbsp tomato sauce
½–1tsp chilli sauce
3–4 tbsp Chinese Stock
(see page 16) or water
2 tsp Cornflour (Cornstarch) Paste (page 16)
a few drops of sesame oil

1 Mix the prawns (shrimp) with the salt, egg white and cornflour (cornstarch) paste.

2 Heat the oil in a preheated wok and stir-fry the prawns (shrimp) for 30–40 seconds only. Remove and drain on paper towels.

3 Pour off the oil and wipe the wok clean with paper towels. To make the sauce, first heat the tablespoon of oil. Add the vegetables and stir-fry for about 1 minute, then add the seasonings with the stock or water and bring to the boil.

4 Add the prawns (shrimp) and stir until blended well. Thicken the sauce with the cornflour (cornstarch) paste and stir until smooth. Sprinkle with sesame oil and serve hot.

Step *2*

Step *3*

Step *4*

Sweet & Sour Prawns (Shrimp)

Use raw prawns (shrimp) if possible; ready-cooked ones can be added to the sauce without the initial deep-frying (step 2).

SERVES 4

INGREDIENTS

300–350 g/10–12 oz raw king or tiger prawns (shrimp) in their shells
vegetable oil for deep-frying
fresh coriander (cilantro) leaves, to garnish

SAUCE

1 tbsp vegetable oil
2 tsp finely chopped spring onions (scallions)
1 tsp finely chopped ginger root
1 tbsp light soy sauce
2 tbsp sugar
3 tbsp rice vinegar
1 tsp Chinese rice wine or dry sherry
125 ml/4 fl oz/½ cup Chinese Stock
(page 16) or water
1 tbsp Cornflour (Cornstarch) Paste (page 16)
a few drops of sesame oil
coriander (cilantro) leaves, to garnish

1 Remove the legs from the prawns (shrimp) but leave the body shell in place.

2 Heat the oil in a preheated wok. Deep-fry the prawns (shrimp) in hot oil for about 45–50 seconds, or until they become bright orange. Remove with a slotted spoon and drain on paper towels.

3 To make the sauce, heat the oil in a preheated wok and add the spring onions (scallions) and ginger, followed by the soy sauce, sugar, rice vinegar, wine and stock or water. Bring to the boil.

4 Add the prawns (shrimp) to the sauce, blend well, then thicken the sauce with the cornflour (cornstarch) paste. Stir until smooth and then add the sesame oil.

5 Serve hot, garnished with coriander (cilantro) leaves.

Step *2*

Step *3*

Step *4*

Baked Crab with Ginger

The crab is interchangeable with lobster. In Chinese restaurants, only live
crabs and lobsters are used, but ready-cooked ones can be used at home.

SERVES 4

INGREDIENTS

1 large or 2 medium crabs,
weighing about 750 g/1½ lb in total
2 tbsp Chinese rice wine or dry sherry
1 egg, lightly beaten
1 tbsp cornflour (cornstarch)
3–4 tbsp vegetable oil
1 tbsp finely chopped ginger root
3–4 spring onions (scallions), cut into sections
2 tbsp light soy sauce
1 tsp sugar
about 75 ml/5 tbsp/⅓ cup
Chinese Stock (page 16) or water
½ tsp sesame oil
coriander (cilantro) leaves, to garnish

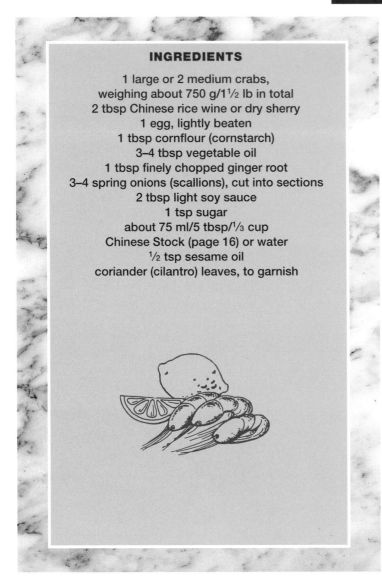

1 Cut the crab in half from the under-belly. Break off the claws and crack them with the back of the cleaver or a large kitchen knife.

2 Discard the legs and crack the shell, breaking it into several pieces. Discard the feathery gills and the stomach sac. Place in a bowl with the wine, egg and cornflour (cornstarch) and leave to marinate for 10–15 minutes.

3 Heat the oil in a preheated wok and stir-fry the crab with ginger and spring onions (scallions) for 2–3 minutes.

4 Add the soy sauce, sugar and stock or water, blend well and bring to the boil. Cover and cook for 3–4 minutes, then remove the cover. Sprinkle with sesame oil and garnish with coriander (cilantro) before serving.

Step *1*

Step *2*

Step *4*

Spiced Scallops

Scallops are available both fresh and frozen.
Make sure they are completely defrosted before cooking.

SERVES 4

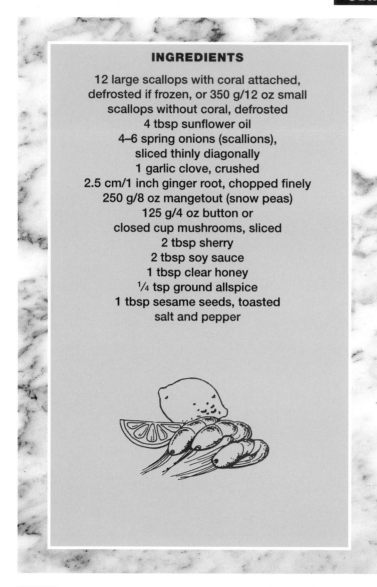

INGREDIENTS

12 large scallops with coral attached,
defrosted if frozen, or 350 g/12 oz small
scallops without coral, defrosted
4 tbsp sunflower oil
4–6 spring onions (scallions),
sliced thinly diagonally
1 garlic clove, crushed
2.5 cm/1 inch ginger root, chopped finely
250 g/8 oz mangetout (snow peas)
125 g/4 oz button or
closed cup mushrooms, sliced
2 tbsp sherry
2 tbsp soy sauce
1 tbsp clear honey
¼ tsp ground allspice
1 tbsp sesame seeds, toasted
salt and pepper

1 Wash and dry the scallops, discarding any black pieces. Detach the corals, if using. Slice each scallop into 3–4 pieces and halve the corals if they are large.

2 Heat 2 tablespoons of oil in the wok, swirling it around until really hot. Add the spring onions (scallions), garlic and ginger, and stir-fry for a minute or so. Add the mangetout (snow peas) and continue to stir-fry for 2–3 minutes. Remove to a bowl.

3 Add the remaining oil to the wok. When really hot add the scallops and corals, and stir-fry for a couple of minutes. Add the mushrooms and continue to cook for a further minute or so.

4 Add the sherry, soy sauce, honey and allspice to the wok, with salt and pepper to taste. Mix thoroughly, then return the vegetable mixture to the wok.

5 Season well and toss together over a high heat for a minute or so until piping hot. Serve immediately, sprinkled with sesame seeds.

Step *1*

Step *2*

Step *3*

Fried Squid Flowers

The addition of green (bell) pepper and black bean sauce to the squid makes a colourful and delicious dish from the Cantonese school.

SERVES 4

INGREDIENTS

350–400 g/12–14 oz prepared and cleaned squid
1 green (bell) pepper,
cored and seeded
3–4 tbsp vegetable oil
1 garlic clove, chopped finely
¼ tsp finely chopped ginger root
2 tsp finely chopped spring onions (scallions)
½ tsp salt
2 tbsp crushed black bean sauce
1 tsp Chinese rice wine or dry sherry
a few drops of sesame oil

1 Open up the squid and score the inside of the flesh in a criss-cross pattern.

2 Cut the squid into pieces about the size of an oblong postage stamp. Blanch in a bowl of boiling water for a few seconds. Drain and dry well on paper towels.

3 Cut the (bell) pepper into small triangular pieces. Heat the oil in a preheated wok and stir-fry the (bell) pepper for about 1 minute. Add the garlic, ginger, spring onion (scallion), salt and squid. Continue stirring for another minute.

4 Finally add the black bean sauce and wine, and blend well. Serve hot, sprinkled with sesame oil.

Step *1*

Step *3*

Step *4*

Fish with Black Bean Sauce

*Any firm steaks such as salmon
or turbot can be cooked by the same method.*

SERVES 4-6

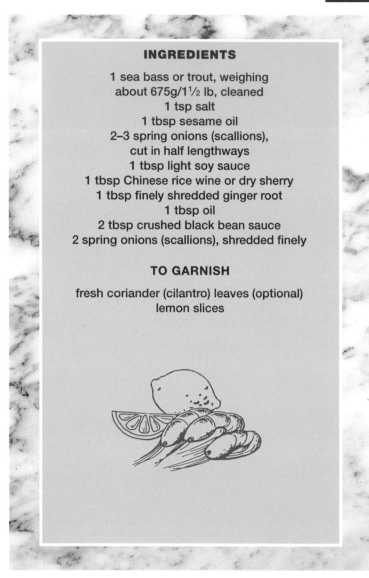

INGREDIENTS

1 sea bass or trout, weighing
about 675g/1½ lb, cleaned
1 tsp salt
1 tbsp sesame oil
2–3 spring onions (scallions),
cut in half lengthways
1 tbsp light soy sauce
1 tbsp Chinese rice wine or dry sherry
1 tbsp finely shredded ginger root
1 tbsp oil
2 tbsp crushed black bean sauce
2 spring onions (scallions), shredded finely

TO GARNISH

fresh coriander (cilantro) leaves (optional)
lemon slices

1 Score both sides of the fish with diagonal cuts at 2.5 cm (1 inch) intervals. Rub both the inside and outside of the fish with the salt and sesame oil.

2 Place the fish on top of the spring onions (scallions) on a heat-proof platter. Blend the soy sauce and wine with the ginger shreds and pour evenly all over the fish.

3 Place the fish on the platter in a very hot steamer (or inside a wok on a rack). Cover and steam vigorously for 12–15 minutes.

4 Heat the oil in a wok or saucepan until hot, then blend in the black bean sauce. Remove the fish from the steamer and place on a serving dish. Pour the hot black bean sauce over the whole length of the fish and place the shredded spring onions (scallions) on top. Serve garnished with coriander (cilantro) leaves, if using, and lemon slices.

Step *2*

Step *3*

Step *4*

Braised Fish Fillets

Any white fish such as lemon sole or plaice is ideal for this dish.

SERVES 4

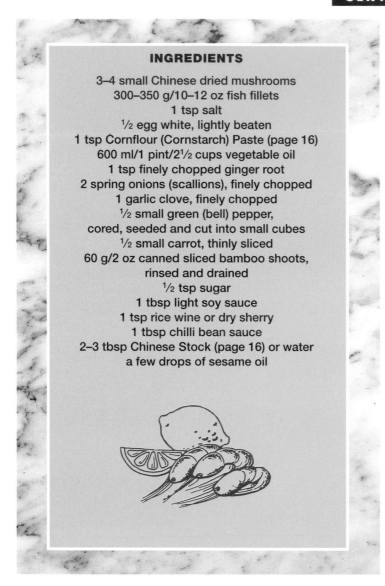

INGREDIENTS

3–4 small Chinese dried mushrooms
300–350 g/10–12 oz fish fillets
1 tsp salt
½ egg white, lightly beaten
1 tsp Cornflour (Cornstarch) Paste (page 16)
600 ml/1 pint/2½ cups vegetable oil
1 tsp finely chopped ginger root
2 spring onions (scallions), finely chopped
1 garlic clove, finely chopped
½ small green (bell) pepper,
cored, seeded and cut into small cubes
½ small carrot, thinly sliced
60 g/2 oz canned sliced bamboo shoots,
rinsed and drained
½ tsp sugar
1 tbsp light soy sauce
1 tsp rice wine or dry sherry
1 tbsp chilli bean sauce
2–3 tbsp Chinese Stock (page 16) or water
a few drops of sesame oil

1 Soak the dried mushrooms in warm water for 30 minutes, then drain on paper towels, reserving the soaking water for stock or soup. Squeeze the mushrooms to extract all the moisture, cut off and discard any hard stems and slice thinly.

2 Cut the fish into bite-sized pieces, then place in a shallow dish and mix with a pinch of salt, the egg white and cornflour (cornstarch) paste, turning the fish to coat well.

3 Heat the oil and deep-fry the fish pieces for about 1 minute. Remove with a slotted spoon and drain on paper towels.

4 Pour off the oil, leaving about 1 tablespoon in the wok. Add the ginger, spring onions (scallions) and garlic to flavour the oil for a few seconds, then add the vegetables and stir-fry for about 1 minute.

5 Add the sugar, soy sauce, wine, chilli bean sauce, stock or water, and remaining salt, and bring to the boil. Add the fish pieces, stir to coat well with the sauce, and braise for another minute. Sprinkle with sesame oil and serve immediately.

Step *3*

Step *4*

Step *5*

Fish in Szechuan Hot Sauce

This is a classic Szechuan recipe. When served in a restaurant, the fish head and tail are removed before cooking.

SERVES 4

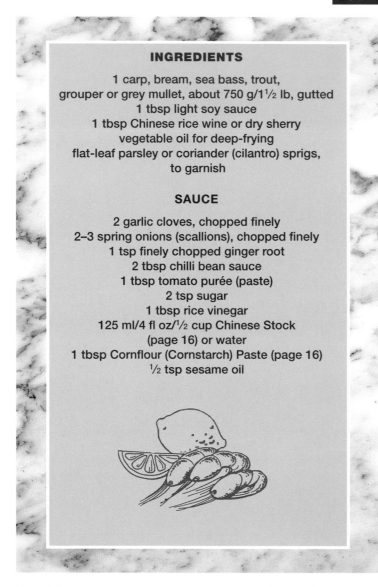

INGREDIENTS

1 carp, bream, sea bass, trout,
grouper or grey mullet, about 750 g/1½ lb, gutted
1 tbsp light soy sauce
1 tbsp Chinese rice wine or dry sherry
vegetable oil for deep-frying
flat-leaf parsley or coriander (cilantro) sprigs,
to garnish

SAUCE

2 garlic cloves, chopped finely
2–3 spring onions (scallions), chopped finely
1 tsp finely chopped ginger root
2 tbsp chilli bean sauce
1 tbsp tomato purée (paste)
2 tsp sugar
1 tbsp rice vinegar
125 ml/4 fl oz/½ cup Chinese Stock
(page 16) or water
1 tbsp Cornflour (Cornstarch) Paste (page 16)
½ tsp sesame oil

1 Wash the fish and dry well on paper towels. Score both sides of the fish to the bone with a sharp knife, making diagonal cuts at intervals of about 2.5 cm/1 inch. Rub the fish with the soy sauce and wine on both sides, then leave on a plate in the refrigerator to marinate for 10–15 minutes.

2 Heat the oil in a preheated wok until smoking. Deep-fry the fish in the hot oil for about 3–4 minutes on both sides, or until golden brown.

3 Pour off the oil, leaving about 1 tablespoon in the wok. Push the fish to one side of the wok and add the garlic, white parts of the spring onions (scallions), ginger, chilli bean sauce, tomato purée (paste), sugar, vinegar and stock. Bring to the boil and braise the fish in the sauce for 4–5 minutes, turning it over once.

4 Add the green parts of the spring onions (scallions) and stir in the cornflour (cornstarch) paste to thicken the sauce. Sprinkle with sesame oil and serve at once, garnished with parsley or coriander (cilantro).

Step *1*

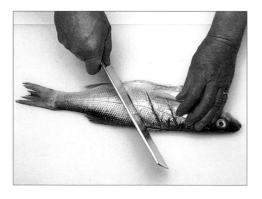

Step *2*

Step *3*

POULTRY DISHES

*Second to pork, poultry is one of the most popular
foods throughout China. It also plays an important
symbolic role. The cock symbolizes the male,
positiveness and aggression; the duck represents
happiness and fidelity; and the pigeon filial concern
and longevity. Duck would be the most popular choice
at a banquet, but chicken, goose and pheasant are also
eaten in quantity.*

*Being uniformly tender, poultry is ideal for Chinese
cooking methods, since these rely on the rapid cooking
of ingredients and small, uniformly-sized pieces of meat.
Poultry can easily be cut into wafer-thin slices, thin
matchstick strips or cubes, and can be quickly cooked
without any loss of moisture or tenderness.*

*Poultry is always purchased live in China, killed at
home and plucked by hand. Since this is not
normally possible in the West, always look for
birds with plump, springy flesh and smooth,
dry skin. The breastbone should be flexible
and springy. It is cheaper to buy a whole
chicken which can then be easily cut into smaller
serving pieces ready for stir-frying, braising
or steaming.*

Aromatic & Crispy Duck

The pancakes traditionally served with this dish take ages to make. Buy ready-made ones from oriental stores, or use crisp lettuce instead.

SERVES 4

INGREDIENTS

2 large duck quarters
1 tsp salt
3–4 pieces star anise
1 tsp Szechuan red peppercorns
1 tsp cloves
2 cinnamon sticks, broken into pieces
2–3 spring onions (scallions),
cut into short sections
4–5 small slices ginger root
3–4 tbsp rice wine or dry sherry
vegetable oil for deep-frying

TO SERVE

12 ready-made pancakes
or 12 crisp lettuce leaves
hoi-sin or plum sauce
¼ cucumber, shredded thinly
3–4 spring onions (scallions), shredded thinly

1 Rub the duck pieces with the salt and arrange the star anise, peppercorns, cloves and cinnamon on top. Sprinkle with the spring onions (scallions), ginger and wine and leave to marinate for at least 3–4 hours.

2 Arrange the duck pieces (with the marinade spices) on a plate that will fit inside a bamboo steamer. Pour some hot water into a wok, place the bamboo steamer in the wok, sitting on a trivet. Put in the duck and cover with the bamboo lid. Steam the duck pieces (with the marinade) over high heat for at least 2–3 hours, until tender and cooked through. Top up the hot water from time to time as required.

3 Remove the duck and leave to cool for at least 4–5 hours – this is very important, for unless the duck is cold and dry, it will not be crispy.

4 Pour off the water and wipe the wok dry. Pour in the oil and heat until smoking. Deep-fry the duck pieces, skin-side down, for 4–5 minutes or until crisp and brown. Remove and drain on paper towels.

5 To serve, scrape the meat off the bone, place about 1 teaspoon of hoi-sin or plum sauce on the centre of a pancake (or lettuce leaf), add a few pieces of cucumber and spring onion (scallion) with a portion of the duck meat. Wrap up to form a small parcel and eat with your fingers. Provide plenty of paper napkins for your guests.

Step *1*

Step *2*

Step *4*

Duck with Pineapple

For best results, use ready-cooked duck meat,
widely available from Chinese restaurants and takeaways.

SERVES 4

INGREDIENTS

125–175 g/4–6 oz cooked duck meat
3 tbsp vegetable oil
1 small onion, shredded thinly
2–3 slices ginger root, shredded thinly
1 spring onion (scallion), shredded thinly
1 small carrot, shredded thinly
125 g/4 oz canned pineapple, cut into small slices
½ tsp salt
1 tbsp red rice vinegar
2 tbsp syrup from the pineapple
1 tbsp Cornflour (Cornstarch) Paste (page 16)
black bean sauce, to serve (optional)

1 Cut the cooked duck meat into thin strips using a Chinese cleaver or very sharp knife.

2 Heat the oil in a preheated wok, add the onion and stir-fry until the shreds are opaque. Add the ginger, spring onion (scallion) and carrot. Stir-fry for 1 minute.

3 Add the duck shreds and pineapple to the wok together with the salt, rice vinegar and the pineapple syrup. Stir until the mixture is blended well.

4 Add the cornflour (cornstarch) paste and stir for 1–2 minutes until the sauce has thickened. Serve hot.

Step *1*

Step *2*

Step *4*

Kung Po Chicken with Cashew Nuts

*Peanuts, walnuts or almonds can be used instead
of the cashew nuts, if preferred.*

SERVES 4

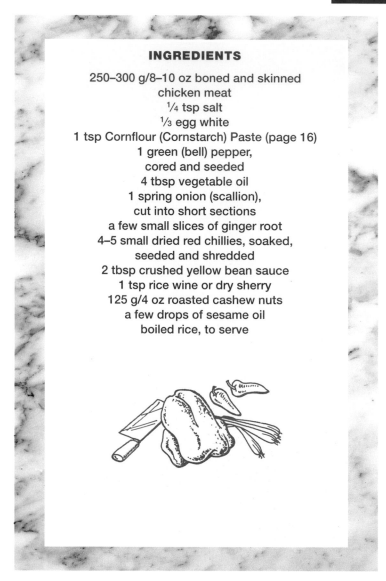

INGREDIENTS

250–300 g/8–10 oz boned and skinned
chicken meat
¼ tsp salt
⅓ egg white
1 tsp Cornflour (Cornstarch) Paste (page 16)
1 green (bell) pepper,
cored and seeded
4 tbsp vegetable oil
1 spring onion (scallion),
cut into short sections
a few small slices of ginger root
4–5 small dried red chillies, soaked,
seeded and shredded
2 tbsp crushed yellow bean sauce
1 tsp rice wine or dry sherry
125 g/4 oz roasted cashew nuts
a few drops of sesame oil
boiled rice, to serve

1 Cut the chicken into small cubes about the size of
sugar lumps. Place in a small bowl and mix with a
pinch of salt, the egg white and the cornflour (cornstarch)
paste, in that order.

2 Cut the green (bell) pepper into cubes or triangles
about the same size as the chicken pieces.

3 Heat the oil in a preheated wok, add the chicken
cubes and stir-fry for about 1 minute, or until the
colour changes. Remove with a slotted spoon and keep
warm.

4 Add the spring onion (scallion), ginger, chillies and
green (bell) pepper. Stir-fry for about 1 minute, then
add the chicken with the yellow bean sauce and wine.
Blend well and stir-fry for another minute. Finally stir in
the cashew nuts and sesame oil. Serve hot.

Step *1*

Step *2*

Step *4*

Chicken with Bean-Sprouts

*This is the basic Chicken Chop Suey to be found in almost every
Chinese restaurant and takeaway all over the world.*

SERVES 4

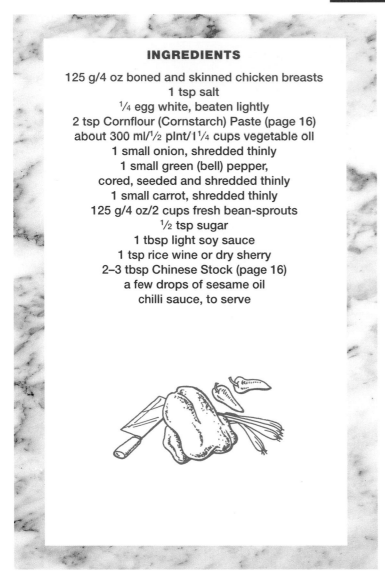

INGREDIENTS

125 g/4 oz boned and skinned chicken breasts
1 tsp salt
¼ egg white, beaten lightly
2 tsp Cornflour (Cornstarch) Paste (page 16)
about 300 ml/½ pint/1¼ cups vegetable oil
1 small onion, shredded thinly
1 small green (bell) pepper,
cored, seeded and shredded thinly
1 small carrot, shredded thinly
125 g/4 oz/2 cups fresh bean-sprouts
½ tsp sugar
1 tbsp light soy sauce
1 tsp rice wine or dry sherry
2–3 tbsp Chinese Stock (page 16)
a few drops of sesame oil
chilli sauce, to serve

1 Thinly shred the chicken and mix with a pinch of the salt, the egg white and cornflour (cornstarch) paste in that order.

2 Heat the oil in a preheated wok and stir-fry the chicken for about 1 minute until no longer pink, stirring to separate the shreds. Remove with a slotted spoon and drain on paper towels.

3 Pour off the oil, leaving about 2 tablespoons in the wok. Add all the vegetables except the bean-sprouts and stir-fry for about 2 minutes. Then add the bean-sprouts and stir for a few seconds.

4 Add the chicken with the remaining salt, sugar, soy sauce and wine. Blend well and add the stock or water. Sprinkle with the sesame oil and serve at once.

Step *2*

Step *3*

Step *4*

Lemon Chicken

*Lemon sauce is a Cantonese speciality, easily available from
Oriental stores, or you can make your own.*

SERVES 4

INGREDIENTS

350 g/12 oz boned and skinned
chicken breasts
1 tbsp rice wine or dry sherry
1 egg, beaten
4 tbsp plain flour blended with 2 tbsp water
vegetable oil for deep-frying
salt and pepper
slices of fresh lemon, to garnish

LEMON SAUCE

1 tbsp vegetable oil
250 ml/8 fl oz/1 cup Chinese Stock (page 16)
1 tbsp caster sugar
1 tbsp lemon juice
1 tbsp cornflour (cornstarch)
1 tsp salt
1 tsp lemon rind

1 To make the lemon sauce, heat the oil in a wok until hot, reduce the heat and add all the other ingredients. Blend well, then bring to the boil and stir until smooth.

2 Cut the chicken into thin slices and place in a shallow dish with wine, and salt and pepper. Leave to marinate for 25–30 minutes.

3 Make a batter with the egg and the flour paste. Place the chicken slices in the batter and turn to coat well.

4 Heat the oil in a wok or deep-fryer. Deep-fry the chicken slices until golden brown, remove with a slotted spoon and drain on paper towels. Cut the chicken slices into bite-sized pieces.

5 Heat about 1 tablespoon of oil in a wok or pan. Stir in the lemon sauce until well blended and pour evenly over the chicken. Garnish with lemon slices.

Step *1*

Step *3*

Step *4*

Peanut Sesame Chicken

*A quick to make chicken and vegetable dish. Sesame and peanuts give it
crunch and the fruit juice glaze gives a lovely shiny coating to the sauce.*

SERVES 4

INGREDIENTS

2 tbsp vegetable oil
2 tbsp sesame oil
500g/1 lb boned and skinned chicken
breasts, sliced into strips
250 g/8 oz broccoli, divided into small florets
250 g/8 oz baby or dwarf sweetcorn,
halved if large
1 small red (bell) pepper,
cored, seeded and sliced
2 tbsp soy sauce
250 ml/8 fl oz/1 cup orange juice
2 tsp cornflour (cornstarch)
2 tbsp toasted sesame seeds
60 g/2 oz/⅓ cup roasted,
shelled, unsalted peanuts
rice or noodles, to serve

1 Heat the oils in a large, heavy-based frying pan or
wok, add the chicken strips and stir-fry until
browned, about 4–5 minutes.

2 Add the broccoli, sweetcorn and red (bell) pepper
and stir-fry for a further 1–2 minutes.

3 Meanwhile, mix the soy sauce with the orange juice
and cornflour (cornstarch). Stir into the chicken and
vegetable mixture, stirring constantly until the sauce has
slightly thickened and a glaze develops.

4 Stir in the sesame seeds and peanuts, mixing well.
Heat for a further 3–4 minutes. Serve at once, with
rice or noodles.

Step *1*

Step *2*

Step *3*

Chicken with (Bell) Pepper

The (bell) pepper can be replaced with celery – the method is exactly the same.

SERVES 4

INGREDIENTS

300 g/10 oz boned and skinned chicken breasts
1 tsp salt
½ egg white
2 tsp Cornflour (Cornstarch) Paste (page 16)
1 green (bell) pepper,
cored and seeded
300 ml/½ pint/1¼ cups vegetable oil
1 spring onion (scallion),shredded finely
a few strips of ginger root, shredded finely
1–2 red chillies, seeded and shredded finely
½ tsp sugar
1 tbsp rice wine or dry sherry
a few drops of sesame oil

1 Cut the chicken breasts into strips, then mix in a bowl with a pinch of the salt, the egg white and cornflour (cornstarch), in that order.

2 Cut the (bell) pepper into thin shreds the same size and length as the chicken strips.

3 Heat the oil in a preheated wok, and deep-fry the chicken strips in batches for about 1 minute, or until no longer pink. Remove the chicken strips with a slotted spoon and keep warm.

4 Pour off the excess oil from the wok, leaving about 1 tablespoon. Add the spring onion (scallion), ginger, chillies and (bell) pepper. Stir-fry for about 1 minute, then return the chicken to the wok. Add the remaining salt, the sugar and wine. Stir-fry for another minute, sprinkle with sesame oil and serve.

Step *2*

Step *3*

Step *4*

Chicken Foo-Yung

A foo-yung dish should use egg whites only to create a very delicate texture. But most people associate foo-yung with an omelette.

SERVES 4

INGREDIENTS

175 g/6 oz boned and skinned chicken breasts,
1 tsp rice wine or dry sherry
1 tbsp cornflour (cornstarch)
3 eggs, beaten
½ tsp finely chopped spring onions (scallions)
3 tbsp vegetable oil
125 g/4 oz green peas
1 tsp light soy sauce
salt and pepper
few drops of sesame oil

1 Cut the chicken across the grain into very small, paper-thin slices, using the cleaver. Place the slices in a shallow dish, add ½ teaspoon salt, pepper, wine and cornflour (cornstarch), and turn in the mixture until they are well coated.

2 Beat the eggs in a small bowl with a pinch of salt and the spring onions (scallions).

3 Heat the oil in a preheated wok, add chicken slices and stir-fry for about 1 minute, making sure that the slices are kept separated. Pour the beaten eggs over the chicken, and lightly scramble until set. Do not stir too vigorously, or the mixture will break up in the oil. Stir the oil from the bottom of the wok so that the foo-yung rises to the surface.

4 Add the peas, soy sauce and salt to taste and blend well. Sprinkle with sesame oil and serve.

Step *2*

Step *3*

Step *4*

Bang-Bang Chicken

The cooked chicken meat is tenderized by beating with a rolling pin,
hence the name for this very popular Szechuan dish.

SERVES 4

INGREDIENTS

1 litre/1¾ pints/4 cups water
2 chicken quarters (breast half and leg)
1 cucumber, cut into matchstick shreds

SAUCE

2 tbsp light soy sauce
1 tsp sugar
1 tbsp finely chopped spring onions
(scallions)
1 tsp red chilli oil
¼ tsp pepper
1 tsp white sesame seeds
2 tbsp peanut butter,
creamed with a little sesame oil

1 Bring the water to a rolling boil in a wok or a large pan. Add the chicken pieces, reduce the heat, cover and cook for 30–35 minutes.

2 Remove the chicken from the pan and immerse it in a bowl of cold water for at least 1 hour to cool it, ready for shredding.

3 Remove the chicken pieces and drain well. Pat dry with paper towels, then take the meat off the bone.

4 On a flat surface, pound the chicken with a rolling pin, then tear the meat into shreds with 2 forks. Mix with the shredded cucumber and arrange in a shallow serving dish.

5 To serve, mix together all the sauce ingredients and pour over the chicken.

Step *1*

Step *2*

Step *4*

Szechuan Chilli Chicken

*In China, the chicken pieces are chopped through the bone for this dish,
but if you do not possess a cleaver, use filleted chicken meat.*

SERVES 4

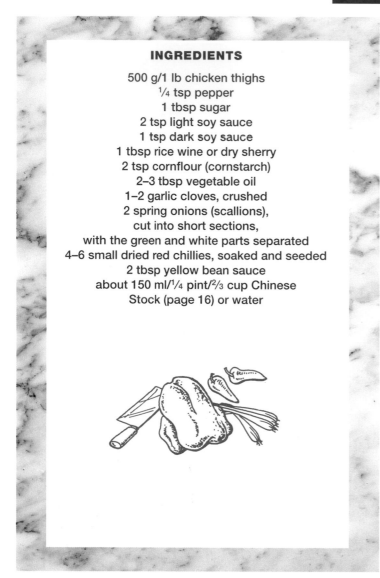

INGREDIENTS

500 g/1 lb chicken thighs
¼ tsp pepper
1 tbsp sugar
2 tsp light soy sauce
1 tsp dark soy sauce
1 tbsp rice wine or dry sherry
2 tsp cornflour (cornstarch)
2–3 tbsp vegetable oil
1–2 garlic cloves, crushed
2 spring onions (scallions),
cut into short sections,
with the green and white parts separated
4–6 small dried red chillies, soaked and seeded
2 tbsp yellow bean sauce
about 150 ml/¼ pint/⅔ cup Chinese
Stock (page 16) or water

1 Cut or chop the chicken thighs into bite-sized pieces. Marinate with the pepper, sugar, soy sauce, wine and cornflour (cornstarch) for 25–30 minutes.

2 Heat the oil in a pre-heated wok, add the chicken pieces and stir-fry until lightly brown for about 1–2 minutes. Remove the chicken pieces with a slotted spoon, remove to a warm dish and reserve.

3 Add the garlic, the white parts of the spring onions (scallions), the chillies and yellow bean sauce. Stir-fry for about 30 seconds, blending well.

4 Return the chicken pieces to the wok, stir-fry for about 1–2 minutes. Add the stock or water, bring to the boil and cover. Braise over medium heat for 5–6 minutes, stirring once or twice. Garnish with the green parts of the spring onions (scallions) and serve immediately.

Step *2*

Step *3*

Step *4*

Chicken with Mushrooms

*Chinese dried mushrooms (shiitake) should be used for this dish –
otherwise use fresh shiitake rather than fresh white mushrooms.*

SERVES 4

INGREDIENTS

300–350 g/10–12 oz boned and skinned
chicken breasts
½ tsp sugar
1 tbsp light soy sauce
1 tsp rice wine or dry sherry
2 tsp cornflour (cornstarch)
4–6 Chinese dried mushrooms,
soaked in warm water for 30 minutes
1 tbsp finely shredded ginger root
salt and pepper
a few drops of sesame oil
coriander (cilantro) leaves, to garnish

1 Cut the chicken into bite-sized pieces and place in a bowl. Add the sugar, soy sauce, wine and cornflour (cornstarch). Leave to marinate for 25–30 minutes.

2 Drain the mushrooms and dry on paper towels. Slice the mushrooms into thin shreds, discarding any hard pieces of stem.

3 Place the chicken pieces on a heat-proof dish that will fit inside a bamboo steamer. Arrange the mushroom and ginger shreds on top of the chicken and sprinkle with salt, pepper and sesame oil.

4 Place the dish on the rack inside a hot steamer or on a rack in a wok filled with hot water and steam over high heat for 20 minutes. Serve hot, garnished with coriander (cilantro) leaves.

Step *1*

Step *2*

Step *4*

Chicken with Celery & Cashew Nuts

Yellow bean sauce, widely available in bottles, gives this quick and easy dish a really authentic taste. Pecan nuts can be used in place of cashews.

SERVES 4

INGREDIENTS

625g/1¼ lb boned and skinned chicken breasts
2 tbsp sunflower or vegetable oil
125 g/4 oz/1 cup (unsalted) cashew nuts
4–6 spring onions (scallions),
sliced thinly diagonally
5–6 celery stalks, sliced thinly diagonally
175 g/6 oz jar yellow bean sauce
salt and pepper
boiled rice, to serve
celery leaves, to garnish (optional)

1 Cut the chicken into thin slices across the grain using a Chinese cleaver or very sharp knife.

2 Heat the oil in the wok, swirling it around until really hot. Add the cashew nuts and stir-fry until they begin to brown, then add the chicken and stir-fry until well sealed and almost cooked through.

3 Add the spring onions (scallions) and celery and continue to stir-fry for 2–3 minutes, stirring the food well around the wok.

4 Add the yellow bean sauce, season lightly and toss until the chicken and vegetables are thoroughly coated with the sauce and piping hot.

5 Serve at once with plain boiled rice, garnished with celery leaves, if liked.

Step *2*

Step *3*

Step *4*

MEAT DISHES

In Chinese cooking, pork is the most popular of all meats. A whole roasted pig, with its skin cracking and burnished, is an essential feature in a Chinese wedding feast or New Year celebration. Lamb is popular in northern China where religious laws forbid the eating of pork. Although it is used in some dishes, beef is less popular with the Chinese than pork. This is partly because of economic and religious issues, but also because beef is less versatile in cooking. Only certain cuts, such as fillet or sirloin, are tender enough for stir-frying. However, these prime cuts tend to dry out and toughen during slow moist cooking. For braising and stewing the most satisfactory cuts are the less tender ones – shin of beef or brisket.

Because pork is tender regardless of cut, it is ideally suited to all Chinese cooking methods. Stir-frying is a simple and easy way of preparing meat, as well as being economical, delicious and healthy. Braising and steaming are also popular methods of cooking meat, ensuring a tender result, and so too is double-cooking. This is a technique in which the meat is first tenderized by long, slow simmering in water, followed by a quick crisping or stir-frying in a sauce – Twice-Cooked Pork (page 158) is a delicious example of this technique.

Beef & Bok Choy

A colourful selection of vegetables stir-fried with tender strips of steak.

SERVES 4

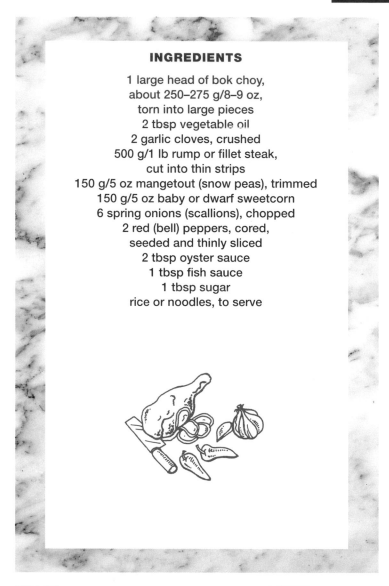

INGREDIENTS

1 large head of bok choy,
about 250–275 g/8–9 oz,
torn into large pieces
2 tbsp vegetable oil
2 garlic cloves, crushed
500 g/1 lb rump or fillet steak,
cut into thin strips
150 g/5 oz mangetout (snow peas), trimmed
150 g/5 oz baby or dwarf sweetcorn
6 spring onions (scallions), chopped
2 red (bell) peppers, cored,
seeded and thinly sliced
2 tbsp oyster sauce
1 tbsp fish sauce
1 tbsp sugar
rice or noodles, to serve

1 Steam the bok choy leaves over boiling water until just tender. Keep warm.

2 Heat the oil in a large, heavy-based frying pan or wok, add the garlic and steak strips and stir-fry until just browned, about 1–2 minutes.

3 Add the mangetout (snow peas), baby sweetcorn, spring onions (scallions), (bell) pepper, oyster sauce, fish sauce and sugar, mixing well. Stir-fry for a further 2–3 minutes until the vegetables are just tender, but still crisp.

4 Arrange the bok choy leaves in the base of a heated serving dish and spoon the beef and vegetable mixture into the centre.

5 Serve the stir-fry immediately, with rice or noodles.

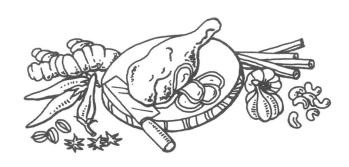

Step *1*

Step *2*

Step *3*

Beef & Chilli Black Bean Sauce

It is not necessary to use the expensive cuts of beef steak for this recipe: the meat will be tender as it is cut into small thin slices and marinated.

SERVES 4

INGREDIENTS

250–300 g/8–10 oz beef steak
(such as rump)
1 small onion
1 small green (bell) popper,
cored and seeded
about 300 ml/½ pint/1¼ cups vegetable oil
1 spring onion (scallion),
cut into short sections
a few small slices of ginger root
1–2 small green or red chillies,
seeded and sliced
2 tbsp crushed black bean sauce

MARINADE

½ tsp bicarbonate of soda (baking soda)
or baking powder
½ tsp sugar
1 tbsp light soy sauce
2 tsp rice wine or dry sherry
2 tsp Cornflour (Cornstarch) Paste (page 16)
2 tsp sesame oil

1 Cut the beef into small thin strips. Mix together the marinade ingredients in a shallow dish, add the beef strips, turn to coat and leave to marinate for at least 2–3 hours – the longer the better.

2 Cut the onion and green (bell) pepper into small equal-sized squares.

3 Heat the oil in a preheated wok. Add the beef strips and stir-fry for about 1 minute, or until the colour changes. Remove with a slotted spoon and drain on paper towels. Keep warm.

4 Pour off the excess oil, leaving about 1 tablespoon in the wok. Add the spring onion (scallion), ginger, chillies, onion and green (bell) pepper and stir-fry for about 1 minute. Add the black bean sauce, stir until smooth then return the beef strips to the wok. Blend well and stir-fry for another minute. Serve hot.

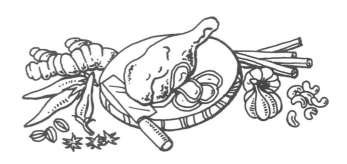

Step *1*

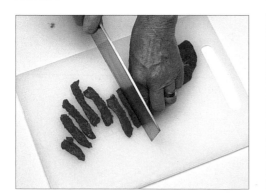

Step *3*

Step *4*

Peppered Beef Cashew

A simple but stunning dish of tender strips of beef mixed with crunchy cashew nuts, coated in a hot sauce. Serve with rice noodles.

SERVES 4

INGREDIENTS

1 tbsp groundnut or sunflower oil
1 tbsp sesame oil
1 onion, sliced
1 garlic clove, crushed
1 tbsp grated ginger root
500 g/1 lb fillet or rump steak,
cut into thin strips
2 tsp palm sugar or demerara sugar
2 tbsp light soy sauce
1 small yellow (bell) pepper,
cored, seeded and sliced
1 red (bell) pepper,
cored, seeded and sliced
4 spring onions (scallions), chopped
2 celery stalks, chopped
4 large open-cap mushrooms, sliced
4 tbsp roasted cashew nuts
3 tbsp stock or white wine
rice noodles, to serve

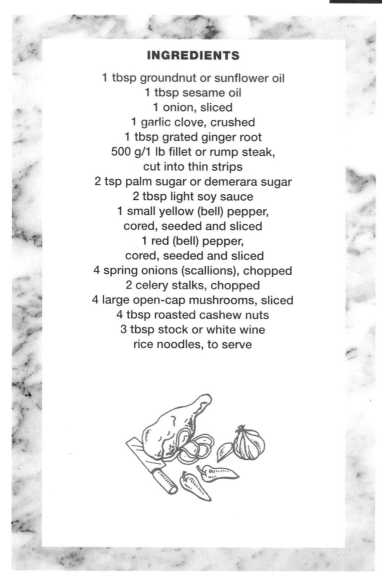

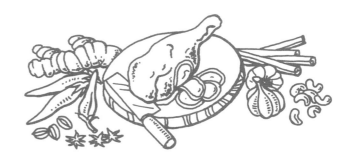

1 Heat the oils in a wok or large, heavy-based frying pan (skillet). Add the onion, garlic and ginger, and stir-fry for about 2 minutes until softened and lightly coloured.

2 Add the steak strips and stir-fry for a further 2–3 minutes, until the meat has browned.

3 Add the sugar and soy sauce, mixing well.

4 Add the (bell) peppers, spring onions (scallions), celery, mushrooms and cashews, mixing well.

5 Add the stock or wine and stir-fry for 2–3 minutes until the beef is cooked through and the vegetables are tender-crisp. Serve immediately with rice noodles.

Step *1*

Step *2*

Step *5*

Red Spiced Beef

A spicy stir-fry flavoured with paprika, chilli and tomato,
with a crisp bite to it from the celery strips.

SERVES 4

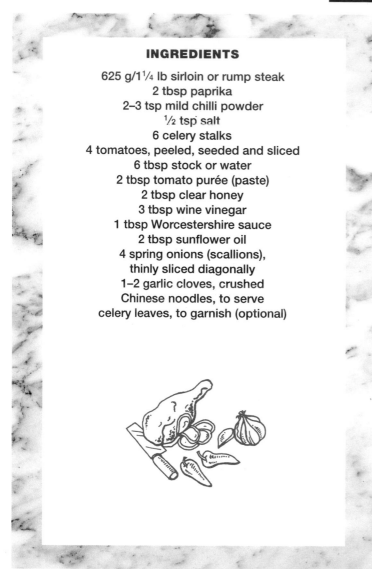

INGREDIENTS

625 g/1¼ lb sirloin or rump steak
2 tbsp paprika
2–3 tsp mild chilli powder
½ tsp salt
6 celery stalks
4 tomatoes, peeled, seeded and sliced
6 tbsp stock or water
2 tbsp tomato purée (paste)
2 tbsp clear honey
3 tbsp wine vinegar
1 tbsp Worcestershire sauce
2 tbsp sunflower oil
4 spring onions (scallions),
thinly sliced diagonally
1–2 garlic cloves, crushed
Chinese noodles, to serve
celery leaves, to garnish (optional)

1 Cut the steak across the grain into narrow strips 1 cm/½ inch thick and place in a bowl. Combine the paprika, chilli powder and salt. Add to the beef and mix thoroughly until the meat strips are evenly coated with the spices. Cover and leave to marinate in a cool place for at least 30 minutes.

2 Cut the celery into 5 cm/2 inch lengths, then slice into strips about 5 mm/¼ in thick. Combine the stock, tomato purée (paste), honey, vinegar and Worcestershire sauce.

3 Heat the oil in the wok, swirling it around until really hot. Add the spring onions (scallions), celery, tomatoes and garlic, and stir-fry for about 1 minute until the vegetables are beginning to soften. Then add the steak strips and stir-fry over a high heat for 3–4 minutes until the meat is well sealed.

4 Add the sauce to the wok and continue to stir-fry briskly until thoroughly coated and sizzling.

5 Serve with noodles and garnish with celery leaves, if liked.

Step *1*

Step *3*

Step *4*

Oyster Sauce Beef

*As in Stir-Fried Pork with Vegetables (page 168), the vegetables
can be varied as you wish.*

SERVES 4

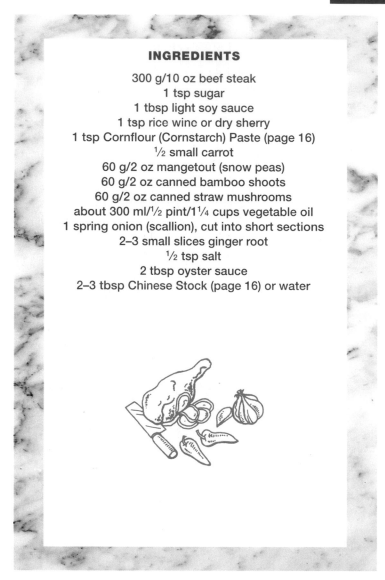

INGREDIENTS

300 g/10 oz beef steak
1 tsp sugar
1 tbsp light soy sauce
1 tsp rice wine or dry sherry
1 tsp Cornflour (Cornstarch) Paste (page 16)
½ small carrot
60 g/2 oz mangetout (snow peas)
60 g/2 oz canned bamboo shoots
60 g/2 oz canned straw mushrooms
about 300 ml/½ pint/1¼ cups vegetable oil
1 spring onion (scallion), cut into short sections
2–3 small slices ginger root
½ tsp salt
2 tbsp oyster sauce
2–3 tbsp Chinese Stock (page 16) or water

1 Cut the beef into small, thin slices. Place in a shallow
dish with the sugar, soy sauce, wine and cornflour
(cornstarch) paste and leave to marinate for 25–30
minutes.

2 Slice the carrots, mangetout (snow peas), bamboo
shoots and straw mushrooms so that as far as possible
the vegetable pieces are of uniform size and thickness.

3 Heat the oil in a preheated wok and add the beef
slices. Stir-fry for about 1 minute, then remove with a
slotted spoon and keep warm.

4 Pour off the oil, leaving about 1 tablespoon in the
wok. Add the sliced vegetables with the spring onion
(scallion) and ginger, and stir-fry for about 2 minutes.
Add the salt, beef, oyster sauce and stock or water. Blend
well until heated through, and serve.

Step *2*

Step *3*

Step *4*

Crispy Shredded Beef

A very popular Szechuan dish served in most
Chinese restaurants all over the world.

SERVES 4

INGREDIENTS

300–350 g/10–12 oz beef steak
(such as topside or rump)
2 eggs
¼ tsp salt
4–5 tbsp plain (all-purpose) flour
vegetable oil for deep-frying
2 medium carrots, shredded finely
2 spring onions (scallions),
shredded finely
1 garlic clove, chopped finely
2–3 small fresh green or red chillies,
seeded and shredded finely
4 tbsp sugar
3 tbsp rice vinegar
1 tbsp light soy sauce
2–3 tbsp Chinese Stock (page 16) or water
1 tsp Cornflour (Cornstarch) Paste (page 16)

1 Cut the steak across the grain into thin strips. Beat the eggs in a bowl with the salt and flour, adding a little water if necessary. Add the beef strips and mix well until coated with the batter.

2 Heat the oil in a preheated wok until smoking. Add the beef strips and deep-fry for 4–5 minutes, stirring to separate the shreds. Remove with a slotted spoon and drain on paper towels.

3 Add the carrots to the wok and deep-fry for about 1–1½ minutes, then remove with a slotted spoon and drain on paper towels.

4 Pour off the excess oil, leaving about 1 tablespoon in the wok. Add the spring onions (scallions), garlic, chillies and carrots, stir-fry for about 1 minute. Add the sugar, vinegar, soy sauce and stock or water, blend well and bring to the boil.

5 Stir in the cornflour (cornstarch) paste and simmer for a few minutes to thicken the sauce. Return the beef to the wok and stir until the shreds of meat are well coated with the sauce. Serve hot.

Step *1*

Step *3*

Step *4*

Lamb & Ginger Stir-Fry

Fillet of lamb (or beef or pork) are cooked with garlic, ginger and shiitake mushrooms. Serve with noodles, or plain boiled rice if preferred.

SERVES 4

INGREDIENTS

500 g/1 lb lamb fillet (tenderloin), or
beef or pork
2 tbsp sunflower oil
1 tbsp chopped ginger root
2 garlic cloves, chopped
6 spring onions (scallions),
white and green parts diagonally sliced
250 g/8 oz shiitake mushrooms, sliced
175 g/6 oz mangetout (snow peas)
1 tsp cornflour (cornstarch)
2 tbsp dry sherry
1 tbsp light soy sauce
1 tsp sesame oil
1 tbsp sesame seeds, toasted
Chinese egg noodles, to serve

1 Cut the lamb fillets into 5 mm/¼ inch thick discs using a very sharp knife.

2 Heat the oil in a wok or frying pan (skillet). Add the lamb and stir-fry for 2 minutes.

3 Add the ginger, garlic, spring onions (scallions), mushrooms and mangetout (snow peas) and stir-fry for a further 2 minutes.

4 Mix the cornflour (cornstarch) with the sherry, add to the wok with the soy sauce and sesame oil and cook, stirring, for 1 minute until thickened. Sprinkle over the sesame seeds and serve with Chinese egg noodles.

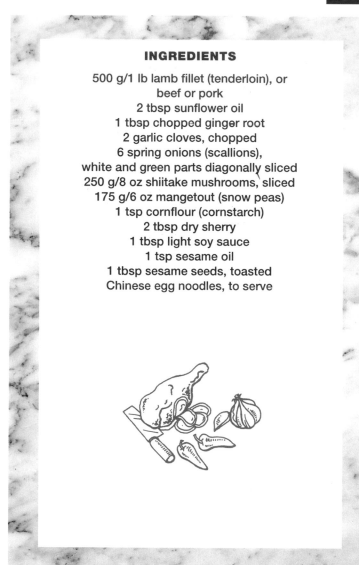

Step *1*

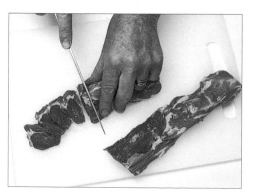

Step *3*

Step *4*

Five-Spice Lamb

Chinese five-spice powder is a blend of cinnamon, fennel, star anise, ginger and cloves. It gives an authentic Chinese flavour to many dishes.

SERVES 4

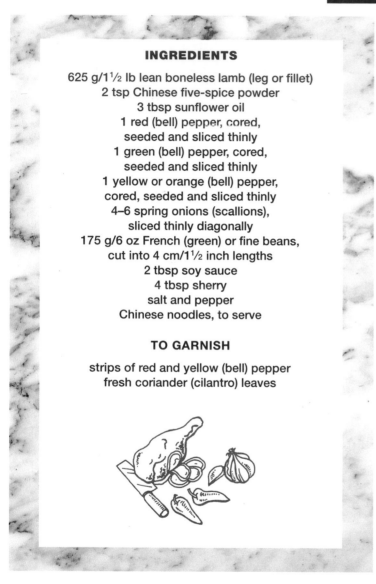

INGREDIENTS

625 g/1½ lb lean boneless lamb (leg or fillet)
2 tsp Chinese five-spice powder
3 tbsp sunflower oil
1 red (bell) pepper, cored,
seeded and sliced thinly
1 green (bell) pepper, cored,
seeded and sliced thinly
1 yellow or orange (bell) pepper,
cored, seeded and sliced thinly
4–6 spring onions (scallions),
sliced thinly diagonally
175 g/6 oz French (green) or fine beans,
cut into 4 cm/1½ inch lengths
2 tbsp soy sauce
4 tbsp sherry
salt and pepper
Chinese noodles, to serve

TO GARNISH

strips of red and yellow (bell) pepper
fresh coriander (cilantro) leaves

1 Cut the lamb into narrow strips, about 4 cm/1½ inches long, across the grain. Place in a bowl, add the five-spice powder and ¼ teaspoon salt, mix well and leave to marinate, covered, in a cool place for at least an hour or up to 24 hours.

2 Heat half the oil in the wok, swirling it around until really hot. Add the lamb and stir-fry briskly for 3–4 minutes until almost cooked. Remove from the pan.

3 Add the remaining oil to the wok and when hot add the (bell) peppers and spring onions (scallions). Stir-fry for 2–3 minutes, then add the beans and stir for a minute or so.

4 Add the soy sauce and sherry to the wok and when hot replace the lamb and any juices. Stir-fry for 1–2 minutes until the lamb is really hot again and thoroughly coated in the sauce. Season to taste.

5 Serve with noodles, garnished with strips of red and green (bell) pepper and fresh coriander (cilantro).

Step *2*

Step *3*

Step *4*

Twice-Cooked Pork

*Twice-cooked is a popular way of cooking meat in China. The meat is
first boiled to tenderize it, then cut into strips or slices and stir-fried.*

SERVES 4

INGREDIENTS

250–300 g/8–10 oz shoulder or leg of pork,
in one piece
1 small green (bell) pepper,
cored and seeded
1 small red (bell) pepper,
cored and seeded
125 g/4 oz canned bamboo shoots,
rinsed, drained and sliced
3 tbsp vegetable oil
1 spring onion (scallion),
cut into short sections
1 tsp salt
½ tsp sugar
1 tbsp light soy sauce
1 tsp chilli bean sauce or freshly minced chilli
1 tsp rice wine or dry sherry
a few drops of sesame oil

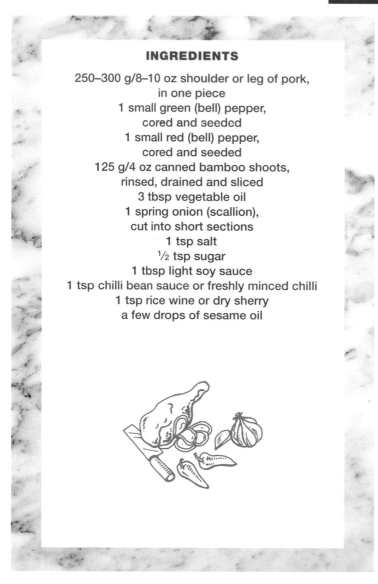

1 Immerse the pork in a pot of boiling water to cover.
Return to the boil and skim the surface. Reduce the
heat, cover and simmer for 15–20 minutes. Turn off the
heat and leave the pork in the water to cool for at least
2–3 hours.

2 Remove the pork from the water and drain well. Trim
off any excess fat, then cut into small, thin slices. Cut
the green and red (bell) peppers into pieces about the
same size as the pork and the sliced bamboo shoots.

3 Heat the oil in a preheated wok and add the (bell)
peppers, bamboo shoots and spring onion (scallion).
Stir-fry for about 1 minute.

4 Add the pork, followed by the salt, sugar, soy sauce,
chilli bean sauce and wine. Blend well, continue
stirring for another minute, then sprinkle with sesame oil
and serve.

Step *1*

Step *2*

Step *4*

Spare Ribs with Chilli

For best results, chop the spare ribs into small bite-size pieces.

SERVES 4

INGREDIENTS

500 g/1 lb pork spare ribs
1 tsp sugar
1 tbsp light soy sauce
1 tsp rice wine or dry sherry
1 tsp cornflour (cornstarch)
about 600 ml/1 pint/2½ cups vegetable oil
1 garlic clove, chopped finely
1 spring onion (scallion),
cut into short sections
1 small green or red chilli pepper,
seeded and sliced thinly
2 tbsp black bean sauce
about 150 ml/¼ pint/⅔ cup Chinese Stock
(page 16) or water
1 small onion, diced
1 green (bell) pepper, cored,
seeded and diced

1 Trim excess fat from the ribs, and chop each one into 3–4 bite-sized pieces. Place the ribs in a shallow dish with the sugar, soy sauce, wine and cornflour (cornstarch) and leave to marinate for 35–45 minutes.

2 Heat the oil in a preheated wok. Add the spare ribs and deep-fry for 2–3 minutes until light brown. Remove with a slotted spoon and drain on paper towels.

3 Pour off the oil, leaving about 1 tablespoon in the wok. Add the garlic, spring onion (scallion), chilli pepper and black bean sauce and stir-fry for 30–40 seconds.

4 Add the spare ribs, blend well, then add the stock or water. Bring to the boil, then reduce the heat, cover and braise for 8–10 minutes, stirring once or twice.

5 Add the onion and green (bell) pepper. Increase the heat to high, and stir uncovered for about 2 minutes to reduce the sauce a little. Serve hot.

Step *2*

Step *3*

Step *5*

Fish-Flavoured Shredded Pork

*'Fish-flavoured' (yu-xiang in Chinese) is a Szechuan cookery term
meaning that the dish contains seasonings normally used in fish dishes.*

SERVES 4

INGREDIENTS

about 2 tbsp dried wood ears
250–300 g/8–10 oz pork fillet
1 tsp salt
2 tsp Cornflour (Cornstarch) Paste (page 16)
3 tbsp vegetable oil
1 garlic clove, chopped finely
½ tsp finely chopped ginger root
2 spring onions (scallions),
chopped finely, with
the white and green parts separated
2 celery stalks, sliced thinly
½ tsp sugar
1 tbsp light soy sauce
1 tbsp chilli bean sauce
2 tsp rice vinegar
1 tsp rice wine or dry sherry
a few drops of sesame oil

1 Soak the wood ears in warm water for about 20 minutes, then rinse in cold water until the water is clear. Drain well, then cut into thin shreds.

2 Cut the pork into thin shreds, then mix in a bowl with a pinch of the salt and about half the cornflour (cornstarch) paste until well coated.

3 Heat 1 tablespoon of oil in a preheated wok. Add the pork strips and stir-fry for about 1 minute, or until the colour changes, then remove with a slotted spoon.

4 Add the remaining oil to the wok and heat. Add the garlic, ginger, the white parts of the spring onions (scallions), the wood ears and celery. Stir-fry for about 1 minute, then return the pork strips together with the sugar, soy sauce, chilli bean sauce, vinegar, wine and remaining salt. Blend well and continue stirring for another minute.

5 Finally add the green parts of the spring onions (scallions) and blend in the remaining cornflour (cornstarch) paste and sesame oil. Stir until the sauce has thickened and serve hot.

Step *1*

Step *3*

Step *4*

Braised Pork & Tofu (Bean Curd)

*The pork used in the recipe can be replaced by chicken or prawns
(shrimp), or it can be omitted altogether.*

SERVES 4

INGREDIENTS

3 cakes tofu (bean curd)
125 g/4 oz boneless pork
1 leek
1–2 spring onions (scallions),
cut into short sections
a few small dried whole chillies, soaked
vegetable oil for deep-frying
2 tbsp yellow bean sauce
1 tbsp light soy sauce
2 tsp rice wine or dry sherry
a few drops of sesame oil

1 Split each cake of tofu (bean curd) into 3 slices crosswise, then cut each slice diagonally into 2 triangles.

2 Cut the pork into shreds. Cut the leek into thin strips. Drain the chillies, remove the seeds using the tip of a knife, then cut into small shreds.

3 Heat the oil in a preheated wok until smoking, then deep-fry the tofu (bean curd) triangles for 2–3 minutes, or until golden brown all over. Remove with a slotted spoon and drain on paper towels.

4 Pour off the hot oil, leaving about 1 tablespoon in the wok. Add the pork strips, spring onions (scallions) and chillies and stir-fry for about 1 minute or until the pork changes colour.

5 Add the leek, tofu (bean curd), yellow bean sauce, soy sauce and wine and braise for 2–3 minutes, stirring very gently to blend everything well. Finally sprinkle on the sesame oil and serve.

Step *1*

Step *3*

Step *4*

Sweet & Sour Pork

This has to be the most popular Chinese dish all over the world.
To vary, replace pork with fish, prawns (shrimp), chicken or vegetables.

SERVES 4

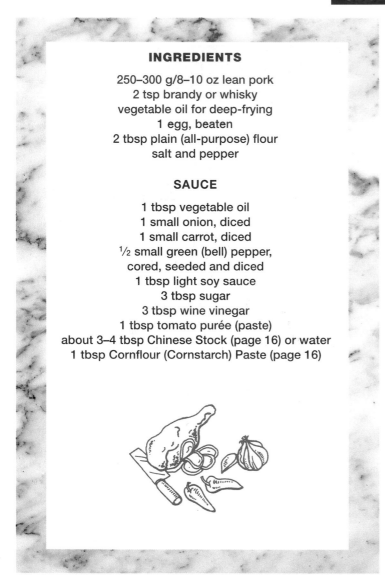

INGREDIENTS

250–300 g/8–10 oz lean pork
2 tsp brandy or whisky
vegetable oil for deep-frying
1 egg, beaten
2 tbsp plain (all-purpose) flour
salt and pepper

SAUCE

1 tbsp vegetable oil
1 small onion, diced
1 small carrot, diced
½ small green (bell) pepper,
cored, seeded and diced
1 tbsp light soy sauce
3 tbsp sugar
3 tbsp wine vinegar
1 tbsp tomato purée (paste)
about 3–4 tbsp Chinese Stock (page 16) or water
1 tbsp Cornflour (Cornstarch) Paste (page 16)

1 Cut the pork into small bite-sized cubes. Place in a dish with the salt, pepper and brandy and leave to marinate for 15–20 minutes.

2 Heat the oil in a wok or deep-fryer. Place the pork cubes in a bowl with the beaten egg and turn to coat. Sprinkle on the flour and turn the pork cubes until they are well coated.

3 Deep-fry the pork cubes in batches for about 3–4 minutes, stirring gently to separate the pieces. Remove with a slotted spoon and drain on paper towels. Reheat the oil until hot, and return the meat to the wok for another minute or so or until golden brown. Remove with a slotted spoon and drain on paper towels.

4 To make the sauce, heat the oil in a pre-heated wok, add the vegetables and stir-fry for about 1 minute. Add the seasonings and tomato purée (paste) with stock or water, bring to the boil and thicken with the cornflour (cornstarch) paste.

5 Add the pork and blend well so that each piece of meat is coated with the sauce. Serve hot.

Step *1*

Step *3*

Step *4*

Stir-Fried Pork with Vegetables

This is a basic 'meat and veg' recipe – using pork, chicken, beef or lamb, and vegetables according to seasonal availability.

SERVES 4

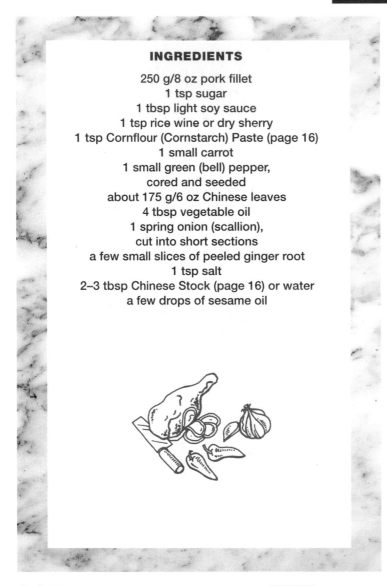

INGREDIENTS

250 g/8 oz pork fillet
1 tsp sugar
1 tbsp light soy sauce
1 tsp rice wine or dry sherry
1 tsp Cornflour (Cornstarch) Paste (page 16)
1 small carrot
1 small green (bell) pepper,
cored and seeded
about 175 g/6 oz Chinese leaves
4 tbsp vegetable oil
1 spring onion (scallion),
cut into short sections
a few small slices of peeled ginger root
1 tsp salt
2–3 tbsp Chinese Stock (page 16) or water
a few drops of sesame oil

1 Thinly slice the pork fillet into small pieces and place in a shallow dish. Add half the sugar, half the the soy sauce, the wine and cornflour (cornstarch) paste, and leave in the refrigerator to marinate for 10–15 minutes.

2 Cut the carrot, green (bell) pepper and Chinese leaves into thin slices roughly the same length and width as the pork pieces.

3 Heat the oil in a preheated wok and stir-fry the pork for about 1 minute to seal in the flavour. Remove with a slotted spoon and keep warm.

4 Add the carrot, (bell) pepper, Chinese leaves, spring onion (scallion) and ginger and stir-fry for about 2 minutes.

5 Add the salt and remaining sugar, followed by the pork and remaining soy sauce, and the stock or water. Blend well and stir for another 1–2 minutes until hot. Sprinkle with the sesame oil and serve.

Step *2*

Step *3*

Step *4*

Fish Aubergine (Eggplant) & Pork

Like Fish-Flavoured Shredded Pork (page 162),
there is no fish involved in this dish.

SERVES 4

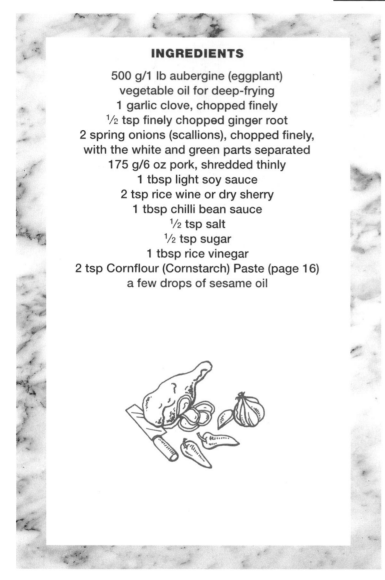

INGREDIENTS

500 g/1 lb aubergine (eggplant)
vegetable oil for deep-frying
1 garlic clove, chopped finely
½ tsp finely chopped ginger root
2 spring onions (scallions), chopped finely,
with the white and green parts separated
175 g/6 oz pork, shredded thinly
1 tbsp light soy sauce
2 tsp rice wine or dry sherry
1 tbsp chilli bean sauce
½ tsp salt
½ tsp sugar
1 tbsp rice vinegar
2 tsp Cornflour (Cornstarch) Paste (page 16)
a few drops of sesame oil

1 Cut the aubergine (eggplant) into rounds and then into thin strips about the size of potato chips – the skin can either be peeled or left on.

2 Heat the oil in a preheated wok until smoking. Add the aubergine (eggplant) chips and deep-fry for about 3–4 minutes, or until soft. Remove and drain thoroughly on paper towels.

3 Pour off the hot oil, leaving about 1 tablespoon in the wok. Add the garlic, ginger and the white parts of the spring onions (scallions), followed by the pork (if using). Stir-fry for about 1 minute or until the colour of the meat changes, then add the soy sauce, wine and chilli bean sauce, blending well.

4 Return the aubergine (eggplant) chips to the wok and add the salt, sugar and vinegar. Continue stirring for another minute or so, then add the Cornflour (Cornstarch) Paste (page 16) and stir until the sauce has thickened.

5 Add the green parts of the spring onions (scallions) and sprinkle on the sesame oil. Serve hot.

Step *2*

Step *3*

Step *4*

VEGETABLE DISHES

Being basically an agricultural country, China has really perfected vegetable cooking to a fine art. The stir-frying technique, in which ingredients are quickly cooked over high heat in a minimum of oil or water, ensures that flavour, texture and colour are preserved, as well as valuable nutrients.

The Chinese eat far more vegetables than meat or poultry, and with few exceptions, almost all meat and poultry dishes include some kind of vegetable as a supplementary ingredient – the idea being to give the dish a harmonious balance of colour, aroma, flavour and texture.

When selecting vegetables for cooking, the Chinese attach great importance to quality. Chinese cooks visit the market on a daily basis to buy fresh produce for the family meal. When selecting vegetables for a Chinese meal, always buy crisp, firm specimens, and cook them as soon as possible.

Another point to remember is to wash the vegetables just before cutting, in order to avoid losing vitamins in water. They should also be cooked immediately after being cut so that the vitamin content is not lost through evaporation.

Sweet & Sour Vegetables

Make your choice of vegetables from the suggested list, including spring onions (scallions) and garlic. For a hotter, spicier sauce add chilli sauce.

SERVES 4

INGREDIENTS

5–6 vegetables from the following:
1 (bell) pepper, seeded and sliced
125 g/4 oz French (green) beans, cut into 2–3 pieces
125 g/4 oz mangetout (snow peas),
cut into 2–3 pieces
250 g/8 oz broccoli or cauliflower florets
250 g/8 oz courgettes (zucchini),
cut into 5 cm/2 inch lengths
175 g/6 oz carrots, cut into julienne strips
125 g/4 oz baby sweetcorn, sliced thinly
175 g/6 oz parsnip or celariac, diced finely
13 celery sticks, sliced thinly crosswise
4 tomatoes, peeled, quartered and seeded
125 g/4 oz button mushrooms, sliced
7 cm/3 inch length of cucumber, diced
200 g/7 oz can water chestnuts or
bamboo shoots, drained and sliced
425 g/14 oz can bean-sprouts, drained
4 spring onions (scallions) sliced thinly
1 garlic clove, crushed
2 tbsp sunflower oil

SWEET & SOUR SAUCE

2 tbsp wine vinegar
2 tbsp clear honey
1 tbsp tomato purée (paste)
2 tbsp soy sauce
2 tbsp sherry
1–2 tsp sweet chilli sauce (optional)
2 tsp cornflour (cornstarch)

1 Prepare the selected vegetables, cutting them into uniform lengths.

2 Combine the sauce ingredients in a bowl, blending well together.

3 Heat the oil in the wok, swirling it around until really hot. Add the spring onions (scallions) and garlic and stir-fry for 1 minute.

4 Add the prepared vegetables – the harder and firmer ones first – and stir-fry for 2 minutes. Then add the softer ones such as mushrooms, mangetout (snow peas) and tomatoes and continue to stir-fry for 2 minutes.

5 Add the sweet and sour mixture to the wok. Bring to the boil quickly, tossing until the vegetables are thoroughly coated and the sauce has thickened. Serve hot.

Step *1*

Step *2*

Step *5*

Stir-Fried Mixed Vegetables

*The Chinese never mix ingredients indiscriminately – they are carefully
selected to achieve a harmonious balance of colours and textures.*

SERVES 4

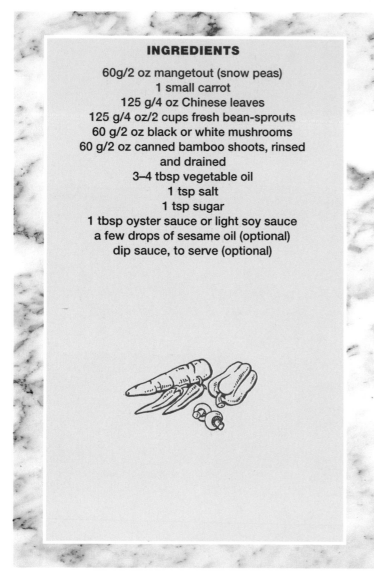

INGREDIENTS

60g/2 oz mangetout (snow peas)
1 small carrot
125 g/4 oz Chinese leaves
125 g/4 oz/2 cups fresh bean-sprouts
60 g/2 oz black or white mushrooms
60 g/2 oz canned bamboo shoots, rinsed
and drained
3–4 tbsp vegetable oil
1 tsp salt
1 tsp sugar
1 tbsp oyster sauce or light soy sauce
a few drops of sesame oil (optional)
dip sauce, to serve (optional)

1 Prepare the vegetables: top and tail the mangetout (snow peas), and cut the carrot, Chinese leaves, mushrooms and bamboo shoots into roughly the same shape and size as the mangetout (snow peas).

2 Heat the oil in a preheated wok, and add the carrot first. Stir-fry for a few seconds, then add the mangetout (snow peas) and Chinese leaves and stir-fry for about 1 minute.

3 Add the bean-sprouts, mushrooms and bamboo shoots and stir-fry for another minute.

4 Add the salt and sugar, continue stirring for another minute, then add the oyster sauce or soy sauce. Blend well, and sprinkle with sesame oil (if using). Serve hot or cold, with a dip sauce, if liked.

Step *1*

Step *2*

Step *4*

Stir-Fried Seasonal Vegetables

*When selecting different fresh vegetables for this dish, bear in mind that
there should always be a contrast in colour as well as texture.*

SERVES 4

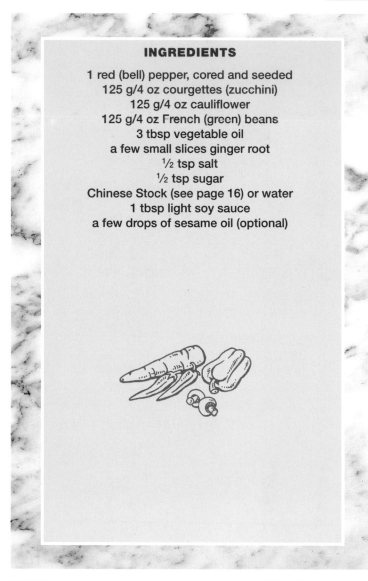

INGREDIENTS

1 red (bell) pepper, cored and seeded
125 g/4 oz courgettes (zucchini)
125 g/4 oz cauliflower
125 g/4 oz French (green) beans
3 tbsp vegetable oil
a few small slices ginger root
½ tsp salt
½ tsp sugar
Chinese Stock (see page 16) or water
1 tbsp light soy sauce
a few drops of sesame oil (optional)

1 Cut the red (bell) pepper into small squares. Thinly slice the courgettes (zucchini). Trim the cauliflower and divide into small florets, discarding any thick stems. Make sure the vegetables are cut into roughly similar shapes and sizes to ensure even cooking. Top and tail the French (green) beans, then cut them in half.

2 Heat the oil in a preheated wok, add the vegetables and stir-fry with the ginger for about 2 minutes.

3 Add the salt and sugar, and continue to stir-fry for 1–2 minutes, adding a little Chinese stock or water if the vegetables appear to be too dry. Do not add liquid unless it seems necessary.

4 Add the soy sauce and sesame oil (if using). Blend well to lightly coat the vegetables. Serve immediately.

Step *1*

Step *1*

Step *2*

Vegetable & Nut Stir-Fry

*A colourful selection of vegetables are stir-fried in a creamy peanut sauce
and sprinkled with nuts to serve.*

SERVES 4

INGREDIENTS

3 tbsp crunchy peanut butter
150 ml/¼ pint/⅔ cup water
1 tbsp soy sauce
1 tsp sugar
1 carrot
½ red onion
4 baby courgettes (zucchini)
1 red (bell) pepper
250 g/8 oz egg thread noodles
30 g/1 oz/¼ cup peanuts, chopped roughly
2 tbsp vegetable oil
1 tsp sesame oil
1 small green chilli, seeded and sliced thinly
1 garlic clove, sliced thinly
200 g/7 oz can water chestnuts,
drained and sliced
175 g/6 oz/3 cups bean-sprouts
salt

1 In a small bowl, gradually blend the peanut butter with the water. Stir in the soy sauce and sugar.

2 Cut the carrot into thin matchsticks and slice the onion. Slice the courgettes (zucchini) on the diagonal and cut the (bell) pepper into chunks.

3 Bring a large pan of water to the boil and add the egg noodles. Remove from the heat immediately and leave to rest for 4 minutes, stirring occasionally to divide the noodles.

4 Heat a wok or large frying pan (skillet), add the peanuts and dry-fry until they are beginning to brown. Remove and set aside.

5 Add the oils to the pan and heat. Add the carrot, onion, courgette (zucchini), (bell) pepper, chilli and garlic, and stir-fry for 2–3 minutes. Add the water chestnuts, bean-sprouts and peanut sauce. Bring to the boil and heat thoroughly. Season to taste. Drain the noodles and serve with the stir-fry. Sprinkle with the peanuts.

Step *1*

Step *3*

Step *5*

Ma-Po Tofu (Bean Curd)

*Ma-Po, the wife of a Szechuan chef, created this dish in the 19th century.
Replace the beef with dried mushrooms to make a vegetarian meal.*

SERVES 4

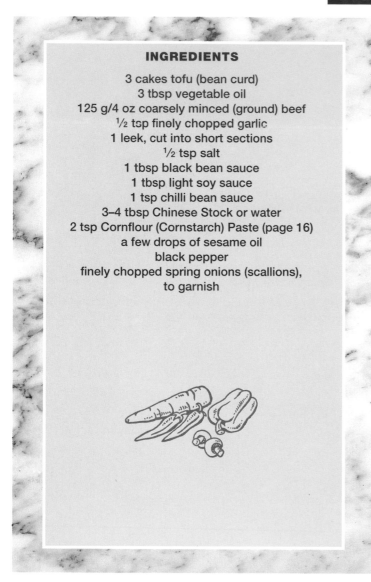

INGREDIENTS

3 cakes tofu (bean curd)
3 tbsp vegetable oil
125 g/4 oz coarsely minced (ground) beef
½ tsp finely chopped garlic
1 leek, cut into short sections
½ tsp salt
1 tbsp black bean sauce
1 tbsp light soy sauce
1 tsp chilli bean sauce
3–4 tbsp Chinese Stock or water
2 tsp Cornflour (Cornstarch) Paste (page 16)
a few drops of sesame oil
black pepper
finely chopped spring onions (scallions),
to garnish

1 Cut the tofu (bean curd) into 1 cm/½ in cubes, handling it carefully. Bring some water to the boil in a small pan or a wok, add the tofu (bean curd) and blanch for 2–3 minutes to harden. Remove and drain well.

2 Heat the oil in a preheated wok. Add the minced (ground) beef and garlic, and stir-fry for about 1 minute, or until the colour of the beef changes. Add the leek, salt and sauces, and blend well.

3 Add the stock or water and the tofu (bean curd). Bring to the boil and braise gently for 2–3 minutes.

4 Add the cornflour (cornstarch) paste, and stir until the sauce has thickened. Sprinkle with sesame oil and black pepper, and garnish with spring onions (scallions).

Step *1*

Step *2*

Step *4*

Tofu (Bean Curd) & Vegetables with Black Bean Sauce

Chunks of tofu (bean curd) are stir-fried with vegetables and black bean sauce. The ingredients can be stir-fried in a wok or cooked in a microwave.

SERVES 4

INGREDIENTS

285 g/9½ oz smoked tofu (bean curd), cubed
2 tbsp soy sauce
1 tbsp dry sherry
1 tsp sesame oil
4 dried Chinese mushrooms,
soaked in warm water for 30 minutes
2 tbsp groundnut oil
1 carrot, cut into thin sticks
1 celery stalk, cut into thin sticks
125 g/4 oz (16–18) baby sweetcorn,
halved lengthwise
1 courgette (zucchini), sliced
4 spring onions (scallions), chopped
125 g/4 oz/1⅓ cups mangetout (snow peas),
each cut into 3 pieces
2 tbsp black bean sauce
1 tsp cornflour (cornstarch)
salt and pepper
1 tbsp toasted sesame seeds, to garnish
egg noodles, to serve

1 Marinate the tofu (bean curd) in the soy sauce, sherry and sesame oil for 30 minutes.

2 Drain the mushrooms, reserving 1 tablespoon of the liquid. Squeeze out excess water from the mushrooms and discard the hard cores. Thinly slice the mushrooms.

3 Heat the groundnut oil in a wok until very hot. Add the carrot, celery and sweetcorn and stir-fry for 2 minutes. Alternatively, place in a large bowl, cover and microwave on HIGH power for 1 minute.

4 Add the mushrooms, courgette (zucchini), spring onions (scallions) and mangetout (snow peas). Stir-fry for 4–5 minutes until just tender. Alternatively, cover and microwave on HIGH power for 4 minutes, stirring every minute.

5 Add the black bean sauce. Mix the cornflour (cornstarch) with reserved mushroom water and stir into the vegetables with the tofu (bean curd) and marinade. Stir-fry, or cover and microwave on HIGH power for 2–3 minutes until heated through and the sauce has thickened slightly. Season to taste. Garnish the vegetables with sesame seeds and serve with the noodles.

Step *1*

Step *2*

Step *4*

Vegetable & Tofu (Bean Curd) Casserole

This colourful Chinese-style casserole is made with tofu (bean curd),
vegetables and black bean sauce.

SERVES 4

INGREDIENTS

6 Chinese dried mushrooms
(or thinly sliced open-cup mushrooms)
275 g/9 oz tofu (bean curd)
3 tbsp vegetable oil
1 carrot, cut into thin strips
125 g/4 oz mangetout (snow peas)
125 g/4 oz/8 baby sweetcorn,
halved lengthways
200 g/7 oz can bamboo shoots,
drained and sliced
1 red (bell) pepper, cut into chunks
125 g/4 oz/1½ cups Chinese leaves, shredded
1 tbsp soy sauce
1 tbsp black bean sauce
1 tsp sugar
1 tsp cornflour (cornstarch)
vegetable oil for deep-frying
250 g/8 oz Chinese rice noodles
salt

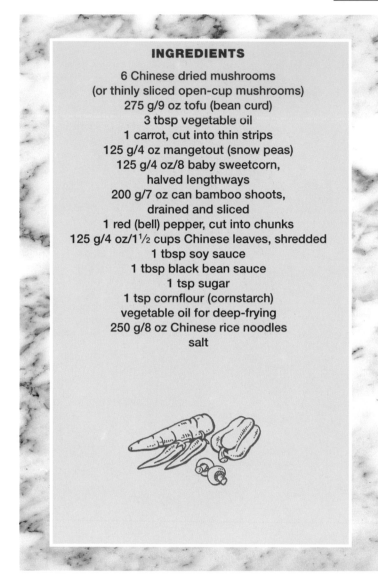

1 Place the dried mushrooms in a small bowl and cover with warm water. Leave to soak for 20–25 minutes. Drain and squeeze out the excess water, reserving the liquid. Remove the tough centres and slice the mushrooms thinly.

2 Cut the tofu (bean curd) into cubes. Boil in a saucepan of lightly salted water for 2–3 minutes to firm up. Drain thoroughly.

3 Heat half the oil in a large flameproof casserole or saucepan. Add the tofu (bean curd) and fry until lightly browned all over. Remove with a slotted spoon and drain on paper towels.

4 Add the remaining oil and stir-fry the mushrooms, carrot, mangetout (snow peas), sweetcorn, bamboo shoots and (bell) pepper for 2–3 minutes. Add the Chinese leaves and tofu (bean curd), and stir-fry for a further 2 minutes.

5 Stir in the soy sauce, black bean sauce and sugar, and season with salt. Add 6 tablespoons of the reserved mushroom liquid (or water if you are using ordinary mushrooms), mixed with cornflour (cornstarch). Bring to the boil, reduce the heat, cover and braise for 2–3 minutes until the sauce has thickened slightly.

6 Heat the oil for deep-frying in a large saucepan. Add the noodles in batches and deep-fry until puffed up and lightly golden. Drain on paper towels and serve with the casserole.

Step *3*

Step *4*

Step *6*

Stir-Fried Mushrooms, Cucumber & Smoked Tofu (Bean Curd)

Chunks of cucumber and smoked tofu (bean curd) stir-fried with straw mushrooms, mangetout (snow peas) and corn in a yellow bean sauce.

SERVES 4

INGREDIENTS

1 large cucumber
1 tsp salt
225 g/7½ oz smoked tofu (bean curd)
2 tbsp vegetable oil
60 g/2 oz mangetout (snow peas)
125 g/4 oz/8 baby sweetcorn
1 celery stalk, sliced diagonally
425 g/14 oz can of straw mushrooms, drained
2 spring onions (scallions), cut into strips
1 cm/½ inch piece ginger root, chopped
1 tbsp yellow bean sauce
1 tbsp light soy sauce
1 tbsp dry sherry

1 Halve the cucumber lengthways. Remove the seeds, using a teaspoon. Cut into cubes, place in a colander and sprinkle over the salt. Leave to drain for 10 minutes. Rinse thoroughly in cold water to remove the salt and drain thoroughly.

2 Cut the tofu (bean curd) into cubes. Heat the oil in a wok or large frying pan (skillet). Add the tofu (bean curd), mangetout (snow peas), sweetcorn and celery. Stir until the tofu (bean curd) is lightly browned.

3 Add the straw mushrooms, spring onions (scallions) and ginger, and stir-fry for a further minute.

4 Stir in the cucumber, yellow bean sauce, soy sauce, sherry and 2 tablespoons of water.

5 Stir-fry for 1 minute before serving.

Step *1*

Step *2*

Step *4*

Money Bags

These steamed dumplings are filled with mushroom and sweetcorn. Try dipping them in a mixture of soy sauce, sherry and slivers of ginger root.

SERVES 4

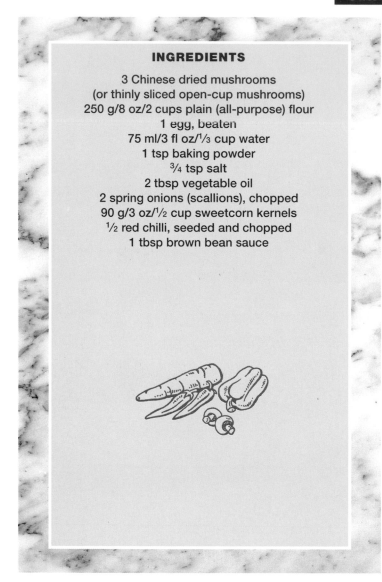

INGREDIENTS

3 Chinese dried mushrooms
(or thinly sliced open-cup mushrooms)
250 g/8 oz/2 cups plain (all-purpose) flour
1 egg, beaten
75 ml/3 fl oz/⅓ cup water
1 tsp baking powder
¾ tsp salt
2 tbsp vegetable oil
2 spring onions (scallions), chopped
90 g/3 oz/½ cup sweetcorn kernels
½ red chilli, seeded and chopped
1 tbsp brown bean sauce

1 Place the dried mushrooms in a small bowl, cover with warm water and leave to soak for 20–25 minutes.

2 To make the wrappers, sift the flour into a bowl. Add the egg and mix lightly. Stir in the water, baking powder and salt. Mix to a soft dough. Knead lightly until smooth on a floured board. Cover with a damp cloth and set aside for 5–6 minutes. This allows the baking powder time to activate, so that the dumplings swell when they are steamed.

3 Drain the mushrooms, squeezing them dry. Remove the tough centres and chop the mushrooms.

4 Heat the oil in a wok or large frying pan (skillet) and stir-fry the mushrooms, spring onions (scallions), sweetcorn and chilli for 2 minutes. Stir in the brown bean sauce and remove from the heat.

5 Roll the dough into a large sausage and cut into 24 even-sized pieces.

6 Roll each piece out into a thin round and place a teaspoonful of the filling in the centre. Gather up the edges, pinch together and twist to seal.

7 Stand the dumplings in an oiled steaming basket. Place over a saucepan of simmering water, cover and steam for 12–14 minutes before serving.

Step *2*

Step *6*

Step *7*

Lentil Balls with Sweet & Sour Sauce

*Crisp golden lentil balls are served in a sweet and sour sauce
with (bell) peppers and pineapple chunks.*

SERVES 4

INGREDIENTS

250 g/8 oz/1 cup red lentils
450 ml/¾ pint/scant 2 cups water
½ green chilli, seeded and chopped
4 spring onions (scallions), chopped finely
1 garlic clove, crushed
1 tsp salt
4 tbsp pineapple juice from can
1 egg, beaten
vegetable oil for deep-frying
rice or noodles, to serve

SAUCE

3 tbsp white wine vinegar
2 tbsp sugar
2 tbsp tomato purée (paste)
1 tsp sesame oil
1 tsp cornflour (cornstarch)
½ tsp salt
6 tbsp water
2 canned pineapple rings
2 tbsp vegetable oil
½ red (bell) pepper, cut into chunks
½ green (bell) pepper, cut into chunks

1 Wash the lentils, then put in a saucepan with the water and bring to the boil. Skim and boil rapidly for 10 minutes, uncovered. Reduce the heat and simmer for 5 minutes until you have a dry mixture. Considerably less water is used to cook these lentils than is normally required, so take care they do not burn as they cook. Stir occasionally.

2 Remove the lentils from the heat and stir in the chilli, spring onions (scallions), garlic, salt and pineapple juice. Leave to cool for 10 minutes.

3 To make the sauce, mix together the vinegar, sugar, tomato purée (paste) sesame oil, cornflour (cornstarch), salt and water, and set aside. Cut the pineapple into chunks.

4 Add the beaten egg to the lentil mixture. Heat the oil in a large saucepan or wok and deep-fry tablespoonfuls of the mixture in batches until crisp and golden. Remove with a perforated spoon and drain on paper towels.

5 Heat the 2 tablespoons oil in a wok or frying pan (skillet). Stir-fry the (bell) peppers for 2 minutes. Add the sauce mixture with the pineapple chunks. Bring to the boil, then reduce the heat and simmer for 1 minute, stirring constantly, until the sauce has thickened. Add the lentil balls and heat thoroughly, taking care not to break them up. Serve with rice or noodles.

Step *1*

Step *4*

Step *5*

Aubergine (Eggplant) in Chilli Sauce

Strips of aubergine (eggplant) are deep-fried, then served in a fragrant chilli sauce with carrot matchsticks and spring onions (scallions).

SERVES 4

INGREDIENTS

1 large aubergine (eggplant)
vegetable oil for deep-frying
2 carrots
4 spring onions (scallions)
2 large garlic cloves
1 tbsp vegetable oil
2 tsp chilli sauce
1 tbsp soy sauce
1 tbsp dry sherry

1 Slice the aubergine (eggplant) and then cut into strips about the size of potato chips (French fries).

2 Heat enough oil in a large heavy-based saucepan to deep-fry the aubergine (eggplant) in batches until just browned. Remove the strips with a perforated spoon and drain on paper towels.

3 Cut the carrots into thin matchsticks. Trim and slice the spring onions (scallions) diagonally. Slice the garlic cloves thinly.

4 Heat 1 tablespoon of oil in a wok or large frying pan (skillet). Add the carrot matchsticks and stir-fry for 1 minute. Add the chopped spring onions (scallions) and garlic, and stir-fry for a further minute.

5 Stir in the chilli sauce, soy sauce and sherry, then stir in the drained aubergine (eggplant). Stir well until the vegetables are thoroughly heated through before serving.

Step *1*

Step *2*

Step *5*

Aubergine (Eggplant) in Black Bean Sauce

*Stir-fried aubergine (eggplant) is served in a black bean sauce with garlic
and spring onions (scallions). Serve with with rice.*

SERVES 4

INGREDIENTS

60 g/2 oz/generous ⅓ cup dried black beans
450 ml/¾ pint/scant 2 cups vegetable
stock
1 tbsp malt vinegar
1 tbsp dry sherry
1 tbsp soy sauce
1 tbsp sugar
1½ tsp cornflour (cornstarch)
1 red chilli, seeded and chopped
1 cm/½ inch piece ginger root, chopped
2 aubergines (eggplants)
2 tsp salt
3 tbsp vegetable oil
2 garlic cloves, sliced
4 spring onions (scallions), sliced diagonally
shredded radishes, to garnish

1 Soak the beans overnight in plenty of cold water. Drain and place in a saucepan. Cover with cold water, bring to the boil and boil rapidly, uncovered, for 10 minutes. Drain. Return the beans to the saucepan with the stock and bring to the boil.

2 Blend together the vinegar, sherry, soy sauce, sugar, cornflour (cornstarch), chilli and ginger in a small bowl. Add to the beans, then cover and simmer for 40 minutes, or until the beans are tender and the sauce has thickened. Stir occasionally.

3 Cut the aubergines (eggplants) into chunks and place in a colander. Sprinkle with the salt and leave to drain for 30 minutes. Rinse well to remove the salt and dry on paper towels.

4 Heat the oil in a wok or large frying pan (skillet). Add the aubergine (eggplant) and garlic. Stir-fry for 3–4 minutes until the aubergine (eggplant) has started to brown.

5 Add the sauce to the aubergine (eggplant) with the spring onions (scallions). Heat thoroughly and garnish with radish shreds.

Step *2*

Step *3*

Step *4*

Gingered Broccoli with Orange

*Thinly sliced broccoli florets are lightly stir-fried and
served in a ginger and orange sauce.*

SERVES 4

INGREDIENTS

750 g/1½ lb broccoli
2 thin slices ginger root
2 garlic cloves
1 orange
2 tsp cornflour (cornstarch)
1 tbsp light soy sauce
½ tsp sugar
2 tbsp vegetable oil

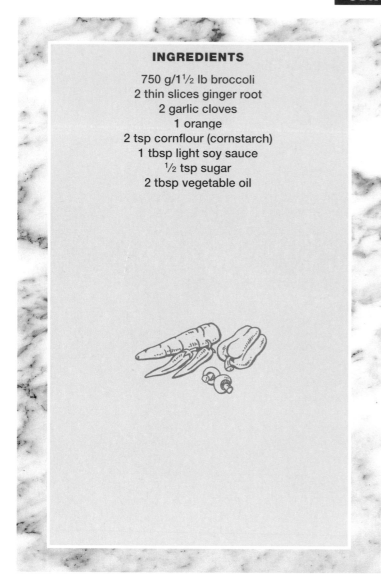

1 Divide the broccoli into small florets. Peel the stems, using a vegetable peeler, and then cut the stems into thin slices. Cut the ginger root into matchsticks and slice the garlic.

2 Peel 2 long strips of zest from the orange and cut into thin strips. Place the strips in a bowl, cover with cold water and set aside. Squeeze the juice from the orange and mix with the cornflour (cornstarch), soy sauce, sugar and 4 tablespoons water.

3 Heat the oil in a wok or large frying pan (skillet). Add the sliced broccoli stems and stir-fry for 2 minutes. Add the ginger root, garlic and broccoli florets, and stir-fry for a further 3 minutes.

4 Stir in the orange sauce mixture and cook, stirring constantly, until the sauce has thickened and coated the broccoli.

5 Drain the reserved orange rind and stir in before serving.

Step *1*

Step *2*

Step *3*

Broccoli in Oyster Sauce

Some Cantonese restaurants use only the stalks of the broccoli for this dish, for the crunchy texture.

SERVES 4

INGREDIENTS

250–300 g/8–10 oz broccoli
3 tbsp vegetable oil
3–4 small slices ginger root
½ tsp salt
½ tsp sugar
3–4 tbsp Chinese Stock
(page 16) or water
1 tbsp oyster sauce

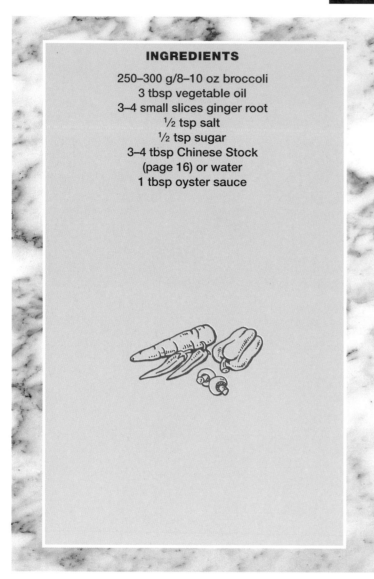

1 Cut the broccoli spears into small florets. Trim the stalks, peel off the rough skin, and cut the stalks diagonally into diamond-shaped chunks.

2 Heat the oil in a preheated wok and add the pieces of stalk and the ginger. Stir-fry for half a minute then add the florets and continue to stir-fry for another 2 minutes.

3 Add the salt, sugar and stock or water, and continue stirring for another minute or so.

4 Blend in the oyster sauce. Serve hot or cold.

Step *1*

Step *3*

Step *4*

Spinach with Straw Mushrooms

Straw mushrooms (available in cans from oriental shops) are served with spinach, raisins and pine kernels (nuts).

SERVES 4

INGREDIENTS

30 g/1 oz/¼ cup pine kernels (nuts)
500 g/1 lb fresh spinach
3 tbsp vegetable oil
1 red onion, sliced
2 garlic cloves, sliced
425 g/14 oz can straw mushrooms, drained
30 g/1 oz raisins
2 tbsp soy sauce
salt

1 Heat a wok or large frying pan (skillet) and dry-fry the pine kernels (nuts) until lightly browned. Remove and set aside.

2 Wash the spinach thoroughly, picking the leaves over and removing long stalks. Drain and pat dry with paper towels.

3 Heat the oil in the wok or frying pan (skillet). Add the onion and garlic, and stir-fry for 1 minute.

4 Add the spinach and mushrooms, and stir-fry until the leaves have wilted. Drain any excess liquid.

5 Stir in the raisins, reserved pine kernels (nuts) and soy sauce. Stir-fry until thoroughly heated and well mixed. Season with salt to taste before serving.

Step *1*

Step *3*

Step *5*

Stir-Fried Bean-Sprouts

Be sure to use fresh bean-sprouts, rather than the canned variety, for this crunchy-textured dish.

SERVES 4

INGREDIENTS

250 g/8 oz/4 cups fresh bean-sprouts
2–3 spring onions (scallions)
1 red chilli pepper (optional)
3 tbsp vegetable oil
½ tsp salt
½ tsp sugar
1 tbsp light soy sauce
a few drops of sesame oil (optional)

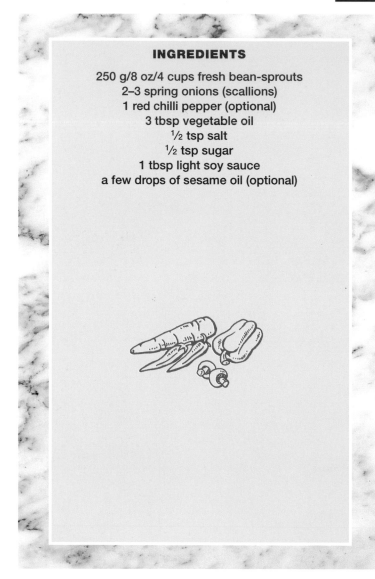

1 Rinse the bean-sprouts in cold water, discarding any husks or small pieces that float to the top. Drain well on paper towels.

2 Cut the spring onions (scallions) into short sections. Shred the chilli pepper, if using, discarding the seeds.

3 Heat the oil in a preheated wok. Add the bean-sprouts, spring onions (scallions) and chilli pepper, if using, and stir-fry for about 2 minutes.

4 Add the salt, sugar, soy sauce and sesame oil, if using. Stir well to blend. Serve hot or cold.

Step *1*

Step *2*

Step *3*

Golden Needles with Bamboo Shoots

*Golden needles are the dried flower buds of the tiger lily. Sold in dried
form at specialist Chinese shops, they give a unique musky flavour.*

SERVES 4

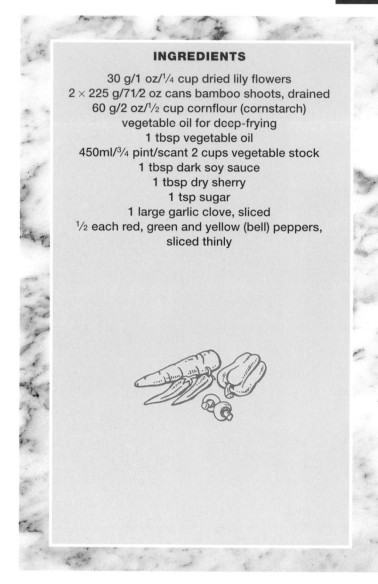

INGREDIENTS

30 g/1 oz/¼ cup dried lily flowers
2 × 225 g/7½ oz cans bamboo shoots, drained
60 g/2 oz/½ cup cornflour (cornstarch)
vegetable oil for deep-frying
1 tbsp vegetable oil
450ml/¾ pint/scant 2 cups vegetable stock
1 tbsp dark soy sauce
1 tbsp dry sherry
1 tsp sugar
1 large garlic clove, sliced
½ each red, green and yellow (bell) peppers,
sliced thinly

1 Soak the lily flowers in hot water for 30 minutes.

2 Coat the bamboo shoots in cornflour (cornstarch).
Heat the oil for deep-frying in a large heavy-based
saucepan. Deep-fry the bamboo shoots in batches until
just beginning to colour. Remove with a perforated
spoon and drain on paper towels.

3 Drain the lily flowers and trim off the hard ends.
Heat 1 tablespoon oil in a wok or large frying pan
(skillet). Add the lily flowers, bamboo shoots, stock, soy
sauce, sherry, sugar and garlic.

4 Add the (bell) pepper to the pan. Bring to the boil,
stirring constantly, then reduce the heat and simmer
for 5 minutes. Add extra water or stock if necessary.

Step *1*

Step *3*

Step *4*

Braised Chinese Leaves

White cabbage can be used instead of the Chinese leaves for this dish.

SERVES 4

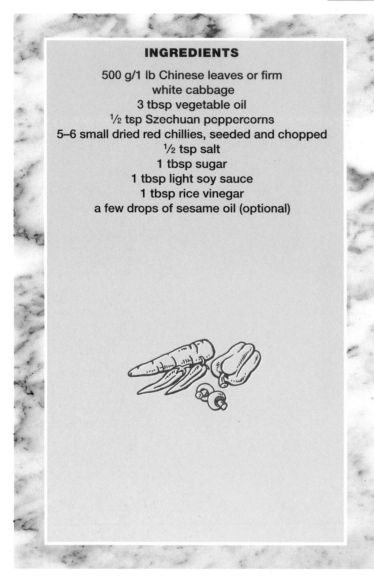

INGREDIENTS

500 g/1 lb Chinese leaves or firm
white cabbage
3 tbsp vegetable oil
½ tsp Szechuan peppercorns
5–6 small dried red chillies, seeded and chopped
½ tsp salt
1 tbsp sugar
1 tbsp light soy sauce
1 tbsp rice vinegar
a few drops of sesame oil (optional)

1 Shred the Chinese leaves or cabbage crossways into thin pieces. (If using firm-packed white cabbage, cut out the thick core before shredding.)

2 Heat the oil in a pre-heated wok, add the Szechuan peppercorns and the dried chillies and stir-fry for a few seconds.

3 Add the Chinese leaves or white cabbage to the peppercorns and chillies, stir-fry for about 1 minute, then add salt and continue stirring for another minute.

4 Add the sugar, soy sauce and vinegar, blend well and stir-fry for one more minute. Sprinkle with the sesame oil, if using. Serve hot or cold.

Step *1*

Step *2*

Step *4*

Lemon Chinese Leaves

These stir-fried Chinese leaves are served with a tangy sauce made of
grated lemon rind, lemon juice and ginger.

SERVES 4

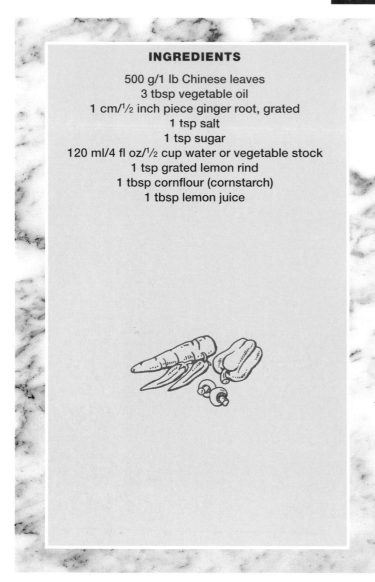

INGREDIENTS

500 g/1 lb Chinese leaves
3 tbsp vegetable oil
1 cm/½ inch piece ginger root, grated
1 tsp salt
1 tsp sugar
120 ml/4 fl oz/½ cup water or vegetable stock
1 tsp grated lemon rind
1 tbsp cornflour (cornstarch)
1 tbsp lemon juice

1 Separate the Chinese leaves, wash and drain thoroughly. Pat dry with paper towels. Cut into 5 cm/2 inch wide slices.

2 Heat the oil in a wok or large frying pan (skillet). Add the grated ginger root, followed by the Chinese leaves, stir-fry for 2–3 minutes or until the leaves begin to wilt. Add the salt and sugar, and mix well until the leaves soften. Remove the leaves with a perforated spoon and set aside.

3 Add the water or vegetable stock to the pan with the grated lemon zest, and bring to the boil. Meanwhile, mix the cornflour (cornstarch) to a smooth paste with the lemon juice, then add to the water or stock in the pan. Simmer, stirring constantly, for about 1 minute to make a smooth sauce.

4 Return the cooked leaves to the pan and mix thoroughly. Arrange on a serving plate and serve immediately.

Step *1*

Step *3*

Step *4*

Chinese Braised Vegetables

This colourful selection of braised vegetables makes a splendid accompaniment to a main dish.

SERVES 4-6

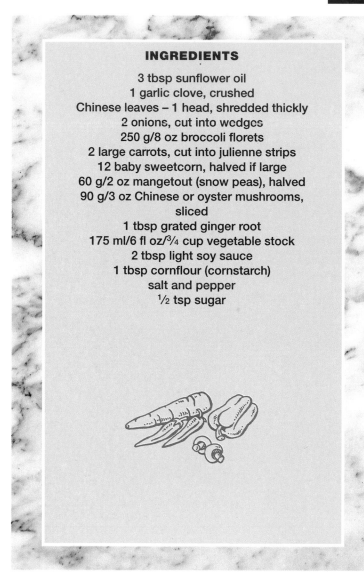

INGREDIENTS

3 tbsp sunflower oil
1 garlic clove, crushed
Chinese leaves – 1 head, shredded thickly
2 onions, cut into wedges
250 g/8 oz broccoli florets
2 large carrots, cut into julienne strips
12 baby sweetcorn, halved if large
60 g/2 oz mangetout (snow peas), halved
90 g/3 oz Chinese or oyster mushrooms, sliced
1 tbsp grated ginger root
175 ml/6 fl oz/¾ cup vegetable stock
2 tbsp light soy sauce
1 tbsp cornflour (cornstarch)
salt and pepper
½ tsp sugar

1 Heat the oil in a large, heavy-based frying pan (skillet) or wok. Add the garlic, Chinese leaves, onions, broccoli, carrots, corn, mangetout (snow peas), mushrooms and ginger and stir-fry for 2 minutes.

2 Add the stock, cover and cook for a further 2–3 minutes.

3 Blend the soy sauce with the cornflour (cornstarch), and salt and pepper to taste.

4 Remove the braised vegetables from the pan with a slotted spoon and keep warm. Add the soy sauce mixture to the pan juices, mixing well. Bring to the boil, stirring constantly, until the mixture thickens slightly. Stir in the sugar.

5 Return the vegetables to the pan and toss in the slightly thickened sauce. Cook gently to just heat through then serve immediately.

Step *1*

Step *2*

Step *5*

Braised Vegetables with Tofu (Bean Curd)

*Also called Lo Han Zhai or Buddha's Delight, the original recipe uses 18
vegetables to represent the 18 Buddhas (Lo Han) – but 6–8 are acceptable.*

SERVES 4

INGREDIENTS

5 g/¼ oz dried wood ears
1 cake tofu (bean curd)
60 g/2 oz mangetout (snow peas)
125 g/4 oz Chinese leaves
1 small carrot
90 g/3 oz canned baby sweetcorn, drained
90 g/3 oz canned straw mushrooms, drained
60 g/2 oz canned water chestnuts, drained
300 ml/½ pint/1¼ cups vegetable oil
1 tsp salt
½ tsp sugar
1 tbsp light soy sauce or oyster sauce
2–3 tbsp Chinese Stock (page16) or water
a few drops of sesame oil

1 Soak the wood ears in warm water for 15–20 minutes, then rinse and drain, discarding any hard bits, and dry on paper towels.

2 Cut the cake of tofu (bean curd) into about 18 small pieces. Top and tail the mangetout (snow peas). Cut the Chinese leaves and the carrot into slices roughly the same size and shape as the mangetout (snow peas). Cut the baby sweetcorn, the straw mushrooms and the water chestnuts in half.

3 Heat the oil in a preheated wok. Add the tofu (bean curd) and deep-fry for about 2 minutes until it turns slightly golden. Remove with a slotted spoon and drain on paper towels.

4 Pour off the oil, leaving about 2 tablespoons in the wok. Add the carrot, Chinese leaves and mangetout (snow peas) and stir-fry for about 1 minute.

5 Now add the sweetcorn, mushrooms and water chestnuts. Stir gently for 2 more minutes, then add the salt, sugar, soy sauce and stock or water. Bring to the boil and stir-fry for 1 more minute.

6 Sprinkle with sesame oil and serve hot or cold.

Step *1*

Step *2*

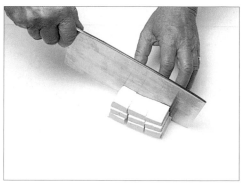

Step *5*

RICE DISHES

Together with noodles, rice forms the central part of
most Chinese meals, particularly in the southern part
of China. In the north, the staple foods tend to be more
wheat-based. Although bland in itself, rice provides a
complementary texture to the other ingredients and
absorbs the stronger flavours of other dishes, making
it an essential and very satisfying part of the
Chinese meal.

For an everyday meal, plain rice is served with two or
three other dishes – usually meat and vegetables
together with a soup. Rice can be boiled and then
steamed, or it can be fried with other ingredients such
as scrambled egg, spring onions (scallions) or peas, then
flavoured with soy sauce.

The most common types of rice used in Chinese cuisine
include white or brown long-grain rice and glutinous
rice. The shorter grain of the glutinous rice has a slight
stickiness when cooked, which makes it ideal for eating
with chopsticks. Rice is also used to make wines,
vinegars, noodles and flour.

Chinese Fried Rice

The rice for this dish may be cooked in the wok or in a saucepan, but it is essential to use cold, dry rice with separate grains for success.

SERVES 4

INGREDIENTS

750 ml/1½ pints/3 cups water
½ tsp salt
300 g/10 oz/1½ cups long-grain rice
2 eggs
4 tsp cold water
3 tbsp sunflower oil
4 spring onions (scallions), sliced diagonally
1 red, green or yellow (bell) pepper,
cored, seeded and thinly sliced
3–4 lean rashers bacon, rinded
and cut into strips
200 g/7 oz fresh bean-sprouts
125 g/4 oz frozen peas, defrosted
2 tbsp soy sauce (optional)
salt and pepper

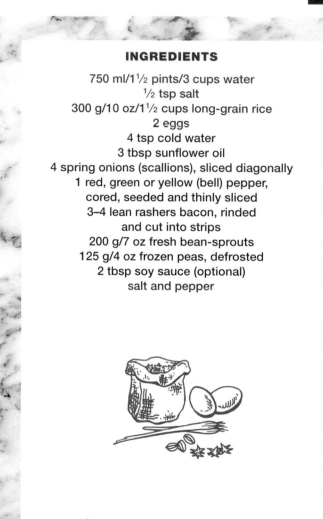

1 Pour the water into the wok with the salt and bring to the boil. Rinse the rice in a sieve under cold water until the water runs clear, drain well and add to the boiling water. Stir well, then cover the wok tightly with the lid or a lid made of foil, and simmer gently for 12–13 minutes. (Don't remove the lid during cooking or the steam will escape and the rice will not be cooked.)

2 Remove the lid, give the rice a good stir and spread out on a large plate or baking sheet to cool and dry.

3 Beat each egg separately with salt and pepper and 2 teaspoons cold water. Heat 1 tablespoon of oil in the wok, swirling it around until really hot. Pour in the first egg, swirl it around and leave to cook undisturbed until set. Remove to a board or plate; repeat with the second egg. Cut the omelettes into thin slices.

4 Add the remaining oil to the wok and when really hot add the spring onions (scallions) and (bell) pepper and stir-fry for 1–2 minutes. Add the bacon and continue to stir-fry for a further 1–2 minutes. Add the bean-sprouts and peas and toss together thoroughly; stir in the soy sauce if using.

5 Add the rice and seasoning and stir-fry for a minute or so. Add the strips of omelette and continue to stir for about 2 minutes or until the rice is piping hot. Serve at once.

Step *1*

Step *3*

Step *4*

Fried Rice with Prawns (Shrimp)

*Use either large peeled prawns (shrimp) or tiger shrimp
for this rice dish.*

SERVES 4

INGREDIENTS

300 g/10 oz/1½ cups long-grain rice
2 eggs
4 tsp cold water
3 tbsp sunflower oil
4 spring onions (scallions),
thinly sliced diagonally
1 garlic clove, crushed
125 g/4 oz closed cup or button
mushrooms, sliced thinly
2 tbsp oyster or anchovy sauce
200g/7 oz can water chestnuts,
drained and sliced
250 g/8 oz peeled prawns (shrimp),
defrosted if frozen
½ bunch of watercress, chopped roughly
salt and pepper
watercress sprigs, to garnish (optional)

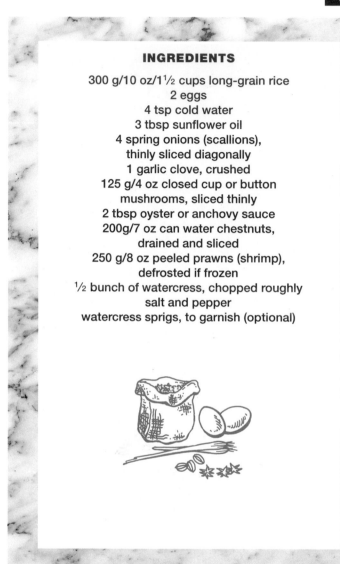

1 Cook the rice in boiling salted water, following the instructions given in Chinese Fried Rice (page 218) and keep warm.

2 Beat each egg separately with 2 teaspoons of cold water, and salt and pepper. Heat 2 teaspoons of oil in a wok, swirling it around until really hot. Pour in the first egg, swirl it around, and leave to cook undisturbed until set. Remove to a plate or board and repeat with the second egg. Cut the omelettes into 2.5 cm/1 inch squares.

3 Heat the remaining oil in the wok and when really hot add the spring onions (scallions) and garlic, and stir-fry for 1 minute. Add the mushrooms and continue to cook for a further 2 minutes.

4 Stir in the oyster or anchovy sauce and seasoning. Add the water chestnuts and prawns (shrimp) and stir-fry for 2 minutes.

5 Stir in the cooked rice and stir-fry for 1 minute. Add the watercress and omelette squares and stir-fry for a further 1–2 minutes until piping hot. Serve at once garnished with sprigs of watercress, if liked.

Step 2

Step 4

Step 5

Egg Fried Rice with Chilli

This version of fried rice is given extra punch with hot red chillies,
spring onions (scallions) and fish sauce.

SERVES 4

INGREDIENTS

250 g/8 oz/1 cup basmati rice
3 tbsp sunflower oil
1 hot red chilli, seeded and chopped finely
2 tsp fish sauce
3 spring onions (scallions) chopped
1 large egg (size 1), beaten
1 tbsp chopped parsley or coriander (cilantro)
1 tbsp soy sauce
1 tsp sugar
salt and pepper

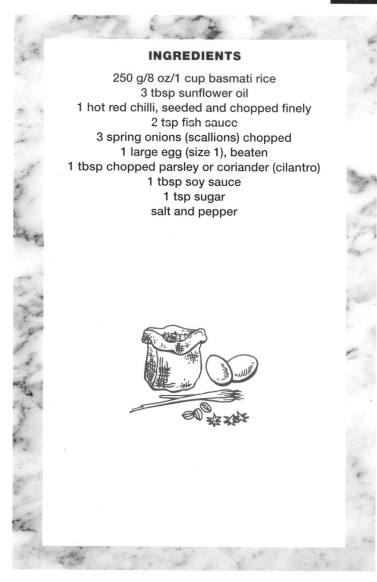

1 Cook the rice in boiling salted water until tender, about 10 minutes. Drain, rinse with boiling water and drain again thoroughly. Spread out on a large plate or baking sheet to dry.

2 Heat the oil in a large, heavy-based frying pan or wok until hot. Add the chilli, fish sauce and spring onions (scallions) and stir-fry for 1–2 minutes.

3 Add the beaten egg and stir-fry quickly so that the egg scrambles into small fluffy pieces.

4 Fork through the rice to separate the grains, then add to the pan and stir-fry for about 1 minute to mix and heat through.

5 Sprinkle a little of the chopped parsley or coriander (cilantro) over the rice. Mix the soy sauce with the sugar and remaining chopped parsley or coriander (cilantro) and stir into the rice mixture, tossing well to mix. Serve immediately.

Step *2*

Step *3*

Step *4*

Fragrant Steamed Rice in Lotus Leaves

The fragrance of the leaves flavours the rice. Lotus leaves are available
from Chinese shops but cabbage or spinach leaves can be substituted.

SERVES 4

INGREDIENTS

2 lotus leaves
4 Chinese dried mushrooms
(or thinly sliced open-cup mushrooms)
175 g/6 oz/generous ¾ cup long-grain rice
1 cinnamon stick
6 cardamom pods
4 cloves
1 tsp salt
2 eggs
1 tbsp vegetable oil
2 spring onions (scallions), chopped
1 tbsp soy sauce
2 tbsp sherry
1 tsp sugar
1 tsp sesame oil

1 Unfold the lotus leaves carefully and cut along the fold to divide each leaf in half. Lay on a large baking sheet and pour over enough hot water to cover. Leave to soak for about 30 minutes or until the leaves have softened.

2 Place the dried mushrooms in a small bowl and cover with warm water. Leave to soak for 20–25 minutes.

3 Cook the rice in plenty of boiling water with the cinnamon stick, cardamom pods, cloves and salt for about 10 minutes – the rice should be partially cooked. Drain thoroughly and remove the cinnamon stick.

4 Beat the eggs lightly. Heat the oil in a wok or frying pan (skillet) and cook the eggs quickly, stirring constantly until set; then remove and set aside.

5 Drain the mushrooms, squeezing out the excess water. Remove the tough centres and chop the mushrooms. Place the drained rice in a bowl. Stir in the mushrooms, cooked egg, spring onions (scallions), soy sauce, sherry, sugar and sesame oil. Season with salt to taste.

6 Drain the lotus leaves and divide the rice mixture into four portions. Place a portion in the centre of each lotus leaf and fold up to form a parcel (package). Place in a steamer, cover and steam over simmering water for 20 minutes. To serve, cut the tops of the lotus leaves open to expose the fragrant rice inside.

Step *1*

Step *4*

Step *6*

Egg Fried Rice

The rice used for frying should not be too soft. Ideally, the rice should have been slightly under-cooked and left to cool before frying.

SERVES 4

INGREDIENTS

3 eggs
1 tsp salt
2 spring onions (scallions), chopped finely
2–3 tbsp vegetable oil
500 g/1 lb/3 cups cooked rice, well
drained and cooled
125 g/4 oz cooked peas

1 Lightly beat the eggs with a pinch of the salt and 1 tablespoon of the spring onions (scallions).

2 Heat the oil in a preheated wok, add the eggs and stir until lightly scrambled. (The eggs should only be cooked until they start to set, so they are still moist.)

3 Add the cold rice and stir to make sure that each grain is separated. Make sure the oil is really hot otherwise the rice will be heavy and greasy.

4 Add the remaining salt, spring onions (scallions) and peas. Blend well and serve hot or cold.

Step *1*

Step *2*

Step *4*

Egg Fu-Yung with Rice

Cooked rice mixed with scrambled eggs, Chinese mushrooms, bamboo shoots and water chestnuts – a great way of using up leftover cooked rice.

SERVES 2–4

INGREDIENTS

175 g/6 oz/generous ¾ cup long-grain rice
2 Chinese dried mushrooms (or
thinly sliced open-cup mushrooms)
3 eggs, beaten
3 tbsp vegetable oil
4 spring onions (scallions), sliced
½ green (bell) pepper, chopped
60 g/2 oz/⅓ cup canned bamboo shoots
60 g/2 oz/⅓ cup canned water chestnuts, sliced
125 g/4 oz/2 cups bean-sprouts
2 tbsp light soy sauce
2 tbsp dry sherry
2 tsp sesame oil
salt and pepper

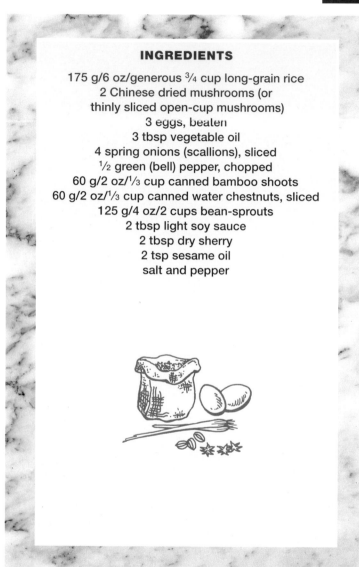

1 Cook the rice in lightly salted boiling water according to the packet instructions. Drain and allow to cool.

2 Place the dried mushrooms in a small bowl, cover with warm water and leave to soak for 20–25 minutes.

3 Mix the beaten eggs with a little salt. Heat 1 tablespoon of the oil in a wok or large frying pan (skillet). Add the eggs and stir until just set. Remove and set aside.

4 Drain the mushrooms and squeeze out the excess water. Remove the tough centres and chop the mushrooms.

5 Heat the remaining oil in a clean wok or frying pan (skillet). Add the mushrooms, spring onions (scallions) and green (bell) pepper, and stir-fry for 2 minutes. Add the bamboo shoots, water chestnuts and bean-sprouts. Stir-fry for 1 minute.

6 Add the rice to the pan with the remaining ingredients. Mix well, heating the rice thoroughly. Season to taste with salt and pepper. Stir in the reserved eggs and serve.

Step *3*

Step *5*

Step *6*

Special Fried Rice with Cashew Nuts

In this simple recipe, cooked rice is fried with vegetables and cashew nuts.
It can be eaten on its own or served as an accompaniment.

SERVES 2–4

INGREDIENTS

175 g/6 oz/generous ¾ cup long-grain rice
60 g/2 oz/½ cup cashew nuts
1 carrot
½ cucumber
1 yellow (bell) pepper
2 spring onions (scallions)
2 tbsp vegetable oil
1 garlic clove, crushed
125 g/4 oz/¾ cup frozen peas, defrosted
1 tbsp soy sauce
1 tsp salt
coriander (cilantro) leaves, to garnish

1 Bring a large pan of water to the boil. Add the rice and simmer for 15 minutes. Tip the rice into a sieve (strainer) and rinse; drain thoroughly and leave to cool.

2 Heat a wok or large frying pan (skillet), add the cashew nuts and dry-fry until lightly browned. Remove and set aside.

3 Cut the carrot in half along the length, then slice thinly into semi-circles. Halve the cucumber and remove the seeds, using a teaspoon. Dice the flesh. Slice the (bell) pepper and chop the spring onions (scallions).

4 Heat the oil in the wok or large frying pan (skillet). Add the prepared vegetables and the garlic. Stir-fry for 3 minutes.

5 Add the rice, peas, soy sauce and salt. Continue to stir-fry until well mixed and thoroughly heated. Stir in the reserved cashew nuts and serve garnished with coriander (cilantro) leaves.

Step *3*

Step *4*

Step *5*

Fried Rice & Prawns (Shrimp)

When you've got one eye on the clock and a meal to make, try this!
Quickly made yet simply stunning to look at, its taste belies its simplicity.

SERVES 4

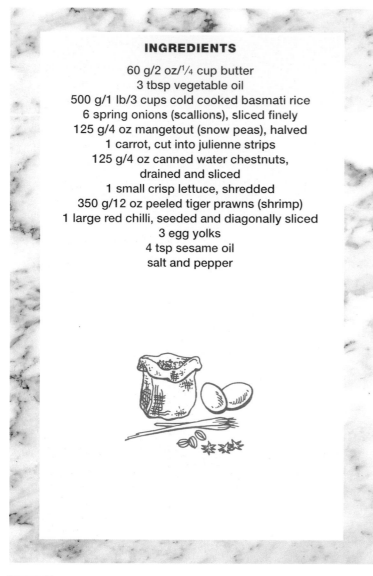

INGREDIENTS

60 g/2 oz/¼ cup butter
3 tbsp vegetable oil
500 g/1 lb/3 cups cold cooked basmati rice
6 spring onions (scallions), sliced finely
125 g/4 oz mangetout (snow peas), halved
1 carrot, cut into julienne strips
125 g/4 oz canned water chestnuts,
drained and sliced
1 small crisp lettuce, shredded
350 g/12 oz peeled tiger prawns (shrimp)
1 large red chilli, seeded and diagonally sliced
3 egg yolks
4 tsp sesame oil
salt and pepper

1 Heat the butter and the oil in a wok or large, heavy-based frying pan (skillet). Add the cooked rice and stir-fry for 2 minutes.

2 Add the spring onions (scallions), mangetout (snow peas), carrot, water chestnuts, and salt and pepper to taste, mixing well. Stir-fry over medium heat for a further 2 minutes.

3 Add the shredded lettuce, prawns (shrimp) and chilli and stir-fry for a further 2 minutes.

4 Beat the egg yolks with the sesame oil and stir into the pan, coating the rice and vegetable mixture. Cook for about 2 minutes to set the egg mixture. Serve at once.

Step *1*

Step *3*

Step *4*

Rice with Crab & Mussels

*Shellfish makes an ideal partner for rice. Mussels and crab add
flavour and texture to this spicy dish.*

SERVES 4

INGREDIENTS

300 g/10 oz/1½ cups long-grain rice
175 g/6 oz crab meat, fresh, canned or frozen
(defrosted if frozen), or 8 fish sticks,
defrosted if frozen
2 tbsp sesame or sunflower oil
2.5 cm/1 inch piece ginger root, grated
4 spring onions (scallions), thinly sliced diagonally
125 g/4 oz mangetout (snow peas), cut into
2–3 pieces
½ tsp turmeric
1 tsp ground cumin
2 × 200 g/7 oz jars mussels, well drained,
or 350 g/12 oz frozen mussels, defrosted
425 g/14 oz can bean-sprouts,
well drained
salt and pepper

TO GARNISH

crab claws or legs (optional)
8 snow peas, blanched

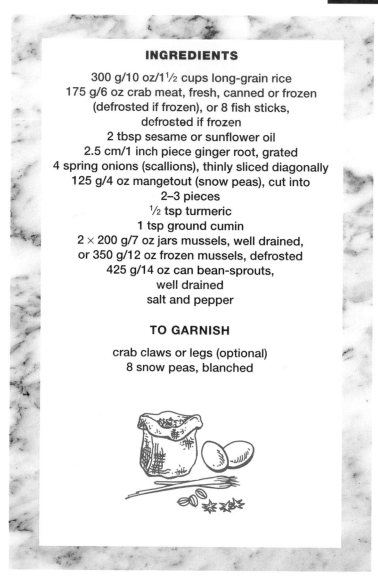

1 Cook the rice in boiling salted water, following the instructions given in Chinese Fried Rice (page 218).

2 Meanwhile, extract the fresh crab meat, if using, and flake. If using fish sticks cut into 3 or 4 pieces.

3 Heat the oil in the wok, swirling it around until really hot. Add the ginger and spring onions (scallions) and stir-fry for a minute or so. Add the mangetout (snow peas) and continue to cook for a further minute.

4 Sprinkle the turmeric, cumin, and seasoning over the vegetables and mix well. Add the crab meat and mussels and stir-fry for 1 minute.

5 Stir in the cooked rice and bean-sprouts and stir-fry for 2 minutes or until really hot and well mixed.

6 Adjust the seasoning and serve very hot, garnished with crab claws and snow peas.

Step *2*

Step *4*

Step *5*

Special Fried Rice with Prawns (Shrimp)

Special Fried Rice, sometimes called Yangchow Fried Rice, is almost a meal in itself. Use completely dry and cold cooked rice for success.

SERVES 4

INGREDIENTS

60 g/2 oz peeled prawns (shrimp)
60 g/2 oz cooked chicken, pork or ham
125 g/4 oz peas
3 eggs
1 tsp salt
2 spring onions (scallions), chopped finely
4 tbsp vegetable oil
1 tbsp light soy sauce
1 tsp Chinese rice wine or dry sherry (optional)
500 g/1 lb/4 cups cold cooked rice

1 Dry the prawns (shrimp) on kitchen paper. Cut the meat into small dice about the same size as the peas.

2 In a bowl, lightly beat the eggs with a pinch of salt and a few pieces of the spring onions (scallions).

3 Heat 2 tablespoons of the oil in a preheated wok. Add the peas, prawns (shrimp) and meat and stir-fry for about 1 minute. Stir in the soy sauce and wine, then remove and keep warm.

4 Heat the remaining oil and add the eggs. Stir to lightly scramble. Add the rice and stir to separate the grains. Add the remaining salt and spring onions (scallions), the prawns (shrimp), meat and peas. Blend well and serve hot or cold.

Step *1*

Step *3*

Step *4*

NOODLE DISHES

In northern China, where wheat grows abundantly, noodles are the mainstay of everyday eating rather than rice. They are temptingly appetizing both in texture and taste. Long noodles are always served at birthday celebrations, and on such occasions the cook will not cut them into shorter lengths because the Chinese believe that the longer they are the longer and happier will be your life.

There are many types of noodles available, both fresh and dried, made from wheat, buckwheat or rice flours. They come in fine threads, strings or flat ribbons, some curled into neat round or oval skeins. You can buy them in oriental food shops or large supermarkets. Like rice, noodles are very versatile – they can be boiled or fried, added to soups, or served plain. Some Chinese like to sprinkle them with salt, pepper, soy sauce, chilli sauce or sesame oil.

Most noodles are prepared in the same way. Because they are precooked as part of the manufacturing process, most noodles need only be soaked in hot water to rehydrate them; sometimes they are boiled or simmered as well. If the packet gives directions on how to cook them, then follow those directions.

Seafood Chow Mein

*Use whatever seafood is available for this delicious noodle dish – mussels
or crab would be suitable.*

SERVES 4

INGREDIENTS

90 g/3 oz squid, cleaned
3–4 fresh scallops
90 g/3 oz raw prawns (shrimp), shelled
½ egg white, beaten lightly
1 tbsp Cornflour (Cornstarch) Paste (page 16)
275 g/9 oz egg noodles
5–6 tbsp vegetable oil
2 tbsp light soy sauce
60 g/2 oz mangetout (snow peas)
½ tsp salt
½ tsp sugar
1 tsp Chinese rice wine or dry sherry
2 spring onions (scallions), shredded finely
a few drops of sesame oil

1 Open up the squid and score the inside in a criss-cross pattern. Cut into pieces about the size of a postage stamp.

2 Soak the squid in a bowl of boiling water until all the pieces curl up. Rinse in cold water and drain.

3 Cut each scallop into 3–4 slices. Cut the prawns (shrimp) in half lengthways if large. Mix the scallops and prawns with the egg white and cornflour (cornstarch) paste.

4 Cook the noodles in boiling water according to the instructions on the packet, then drain and rinse under cold water. Drain well, then toss with 1 tablespoon of oil.

5 Heat 3 tablespoons of oil in a preheated wok. Add the noodles and 1 tablespoon of the soy sauce and stir-fry for 2–3 minutes. Remove to a large serving dish.

6 Heat the remaining oil in the wok and add the mangetout (snow peas) and seafood. Stir-fry for about 2 minutes, then add the salt, sugar, wine, remaining soy sauce and about half the spring onions (scallions). Blend well and add a little stock or water if necessary.

7 Pour the seafood mixture on top of the noodles and sprinkle with sesame oil. Garnish with the remaining spring onions (scallions) and serve hot or cold.

Step *1*

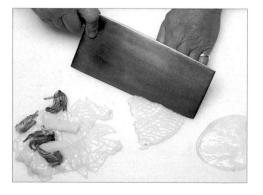

Step *3*

Step *5*

Chicken or Pork Chow Mein

This is a basic recipe – the meat and/or vegetables can be varied as much as you like.

SERVES 4

INGREDIENTS

250 g/8 oz egg noodles
4–5 tbsp vegetable oil
125 g/4 oz French (green) beans
250 g/8 oz cooked chicken breasts,
or pork fillet
2 tbsp light soy sauce
1 tsp salt
½ tsp sugar
1 tbsp Chinese rice wine or dry sherry
2 spring onions (scallions), shredded finely
a few drops of sesame oil
chilli sauce, to serve (optional)

1 Cook the noodles in boiling water according to the instructions on the packet. Drain and rinse under cold water. Drain again then toss with 1 tablespoon of the oil.

2 Slice the meat into thin shreds. Top and tail the beans.

3 Heat 3 tablespoons of oil in a preheated wok until hot, add the noodles and stir-fry for 2–3 minutes with 1 tablespoon soy sauce, then remove to a serving dish. Keep warm.

4 Heat the remaining oil and stir-fry the beans and meat for about 2 minutes. Add the salt, sugar, wine, the remaining soy sauce and about half the spring onions (scallions) to the wok.

5 Blend the meat mixture well and add a little stock if necessary, then pour on top of the noodles, and sprinkle with sesame oil and the remaining spring onions (scallions). Serve hot or cold with or without chilli sauce.

Step *1*

Step *3*

Step *4*

Chicken Chow Mein

A quick stir-fry of chicken and mixed vegetables which is mixed with
Chinese egg noodles and a dash of sesame oil.

SERVES 4

INGREDIENTS

250g/8oz egg noodles
175 g/6 oz broccoli florets
2 tbsp sunflower oil
1 garlic clove, sliced
2.5 cm/1 inch piece ginger root, chopped
250 g/8 oz boned and skinned
chicken breasts, shredded finely
1 onion, sliced
125 g/4 oz shiitake mushrooms
1 red (bell) pepper
1 tsp cornflour (cornstarch)
2 tbsp sherry
250 g/8 oz baby sweetcorn,
drained and halved lengthwise
2 tbsp soy sauce
1 tsp sesame oil
2 tbsp sesame seeds, roasted

28 syns

1 Put the noodles in a bowl, pour over boiling water and leave to stand for 4 minutes. Drain thoroughly.

2 Meanwhile, blanch the broccoli in boiling salted water for 2 minutes, then drain.

3 Heat the oil in a wok or large frying pan (skillet), add the garlic, ginger, chicken and onion and stir-fry for 2 minutes until the chicken strips are sealed and the onion softened.

4 Add the broccoli, mushrooms and red (bell) pepper and stir-fry for a further 2 minutes.

5 Mix the cornflour (cornstarch) with the sherry then stir into the pan with the sweetcorn, sherry mixture, soy sauce, drained noodles and sesame oil and heat through, stirring, until thickened. Sprinkle over the sesame seeds.

Step *1*

Step *4*

Step *5*

Singapore-Style Rice Noodles

Rice noodles, or vermicelli, are also known as rice sticks. Egg noodles can be used for this dish, but it will not taste the same.

SERVES 4

INGREDIENTS

200 g/7 oz rice vermicelli
125 g/4 oz cooked chicken or pork
60 g/2 oz peeled prawns (shrimp),
defrosted if frozen
4 tbsp vegetable oil
1 onion, shredded thinly
125 g/4 oz/2 cups fresh bean-sprouts
1 tsp salt
1 tbsp mild curry powder
2 tbsp light soy sauce
2 spring onions (scallions), shredded thinly
1–2 small fresh green or red chilli peppers,
seeded and shredded thinly

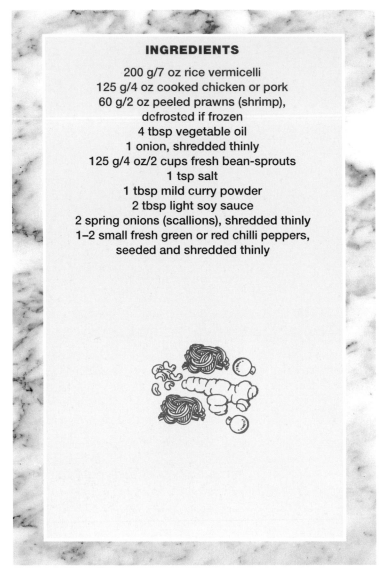

1 Soak the rice vermicelli in boiling water for 8–10 minutes, then rinse in cold water and drain well.

2 Thinly slice the cooked meat. Dry the prawns (shrimp) on paper towels.

3 Heat the oil in a preheated wok. Add the onion and stir-fry until opaque. Add the bean-sprouts and stir-fry for 1 minute.

4 Add the noodles with the meat and prawns (shrimp), and continue stirring for another minute.

5 Blend in the salt, curry powder and soy sauce, followed by the spring onions (scallions) and chilli peppers. Stir-fry for one more minute, then serve immediately.

Step *1*

Step *2*

Step *4*

Mixed Vegetable Chow Mein

Egg noodles are fried with a colourful variety of vegetables to make this well-known dish.

SERVES 4

INGREDIENTS

500 g/1 lb egg noodles
4 tbsp vegetable oil
1 onion, sliced thinly
2 carrots, cut into thin sticks
125 g/4 oz/1⅓ cups button mushrooms,
quartered
125 g/4 oz mangetout (snow peas)
½ cucumber, cut into sticks
125 g/4 oz/2 cups spinach, shredded
125 g/4 oz/2 cups fresh bean-sprouts
2 tbsp dark soy sauce
1 tbsp sherry
1 tsp salt
1 tsp sugar
1 tsp cornflour (cornstarch)
1 tsp sesame oil

1 Cook the noodles according to the packet instructions. Drain and rinse under running cold water until cool. Set aside.

2 Heat 3 tablespoons of the vegetable oil in a wok or large frying pan (skillet). Add the onion and carrots, and stir-fry for 1 minute. Add the mushrooms, mangetout (snow peas) and cucumber, and stir-fry for a further minute.

3 Stir in the remaining vegetable oil and add the drained noodles with the spinach and bean-sprouts.

4 Blend together the remaining ingredients and pour over the noodles and vegetables.

5 Stir-fry until thoroughly heated and serve.

Step *2*

Step *3*

Step *4*

Chow Mein

This is a basic recipe for Chow Mein. Additional ingredients such as chicken or pork can be added if liked.

SERVES 4

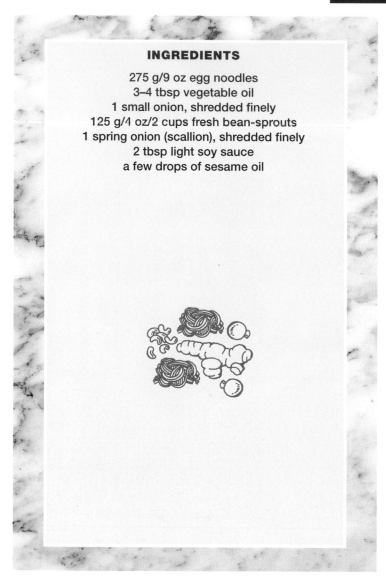

INGREDIENTS

275 g/9 oz egg noodles
3–4 tbsp vegetable oil
1 small onion, shredded finely
125 g/4 oz/2 cups fresh bean-sprouts
1 spring onion (scallion), shredded finely
2 tbsp light soy sauce
a few drops of sesame oil

1 Cook the noodles in salted boiling water according to the instructions on the packet.

2 Drain and rinse the noodles in cold water; drain well, then toss with a little vegetable oil.

3 Heat the remaining oil in a preheated wok. Stir-fry the onion for about 30–40 seconds, then add the bean-sprouts and noodles, stir and toss for 1 more minute.

4 Add the spring onion (scallion) and soy sauce and blend well. Sprinkle with the sesame oil and serve.

Step *1*

Step *3*

Step *4*

Homemade Noodles with Stir-Fried Vegetables

These noodles are simple to make; you do not need a pasta-making machine as they are rolled out by hand.

SERVES 4

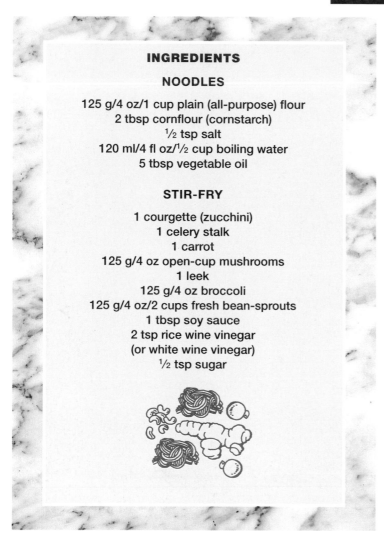

INGREDIENTS

NOODLES

125 g/4 oz/1 cup plain (all-purpose) flour
2 tbsp cornflour (cornstarch)
½ tsp salt
120 ml/4 fl oz/½ cup boiling water
5 tbsp vegetable oil

STIR-FRY

1 courgette (zucchini)
1 celery stalk
1 carrot
125 g/4 oz open-cup mushrooms
1 leek
125 g/4 oz broccoli
125 g/4 oz/2 cups fresh bean-sprouts
1 tbsp soy sauce
2 tsp rice wine vinegar
(or white wine vinegar)
½ tsp sugar

1 To prepare the noodles, sift the flour, cornflour (cornstarch) and salt into a bowl. Make a well in the centre and pour in the boiling water and 1 teaspoon of the oil. Mix quickly, using a wooden spoon, to make a soft dough. Cover and leave for 5–6 minutes.

2 Prepare the vegetables for the stir-fry. Cut the courgette (zucchini), celery and carrot into thin sticks. Slice the mushrooms and leek. Divide the broccoli into small florets, peel and thinly slice the stalks.

3 Make the noodles by rolling small balls of dough across a very lightly oiled work surface (counter) with the palm of your hand to form thin noodles. Do not worry if some of the noodles break. Set aside.

4 Heat 3 tablespoons of oil in a wok or large frying pan (skillet). Add the noodles in batches and fry over a high heat for 1 minute. Reduce the heat and cook for a further 2 minutes. Remove and drain on paper towels.

5 Heat the remaining oil in the pan. Add the courgette (zucchini), celery and carrot, and stir-fry for 1 minute. Add the mushrooms, broccoli and leek, and stir-fry for a further minute. Stir in the remaining ingredients and mix well until thoroughly heated.

6 Add the noodles and toss to mix together over a high heat. Serve immediately.

Step *3*

Step *4*

Step *5*

INDEX